MOUNTAIN MONARCHS
BIGHORN SHEEP

NorthWord®
WILDLIFE SERIES

DEDICATION
In memory of Mrs. Lucille Ayers. Hey, Aunt Lucy;
we're still smiling about your naturally natural "Windy Stories."

Book design by Russell S. Kuepper

NorthWord Press
5900 Green Oak Drive
Minnetonka, MN 55343
1-800-328-3895

Library of Congress Cataloging-in-Publication Data
Gildart, Robert C.
    Bighorn sheep : mountain monarchs / by Robert C. Gildart.
    p. cm. - (NorthWord wildlife series)
Includes bibliographical references (p.   ) and index.
ISBN 1-55971-641-X (paperback)
1. Bighorn sheep. I. Title. II. Series.
QL737.U53 G53 1997
599.649 - dc21   97-7753
                                        CIP

Printed in Malaysia

MOUNTAIN MONARCHS
BIGHORN SHEEP

by Bert Gildart

NorthWord®
NorthWord Press
Minnetonka, Minnesota

ACKNOWLEDGMENTS

Over the past few years, many people have helped me increase my understanding and hence my appreciation of mountain sheep. And though this book is relatively small, often their contributions were relatively large and sometimes bespoke decades of experience with a complex animal. The following helped, and often in ways too numerous to detail here.

Naturalist Dick Coe, who spoke with me at length about predation and food habits of the Mummy Range herd in Rocky Mountain National Park; Biologist Joe Crestco, who drove with me through ideal sheep habitat near Moab, Utah, today only tenuously occupied; Montana Biologist Denis Flath and Nevada Biologist Craig Stevenson, who both helped me understand the complexities of aging horns; Ecologist Jerry Freilich, who introduced me to various techniques for identifying sheep that do not involve tagging or collaring; Terrestrial Ecologist Mark Jorgensen, who helped me understand the immense "Battle at Beringia"; Biologist Kim Keating, who reviewed several sections of my manuscript and provided valuable comment; June Sampson, Director of the National Bighorn Sheep Center in Dubois, Wyoming, who opened the Center's research facilities and introduced me to other sheep enthusiasts; Biologist John McCarthy, who hiked with me on a sheep range near Augusta, Montana, and educated me about the animal's food habitats; Biologist Bruce Sterling, who visited with me about lamb and ewe mortality; Jim Deforge, who provided me a tour of the Desert Bighorn Sheep Institute; and John Fraley, an author as well as a state Information & Education Officer, who reviewed my manuscript.

I'd also like to thank all those gracious and generous "upstairs" librarians at the Flathead County Library; and Glacier's Resource Management Specialist, Bruce Fladmark, who authorized extensive use of the park library.

A particular note of gratitude goes to NorthWord Editor, Barbara Harold, for her encouragement, faith in the project, and for asking questions that provided what I hope may be a better balanced treatise. I'd like to thank my mother and father for instilling in me an intellectual appreciation of the world that surrounds us; and my Aunt Sharlette, who pointed me west so long ago. I'd like to thank Angie and David; forced as children to get down on their hands and knees and help me differentiate between goat scat, sheep scat, and deer scat. And last, but not least, I simply must thank Janie, my wife and front-line reader, who climbed literal and figurative mountains as we learned more about the majesty of mountain sheep.

The horn was "a fathom long" wrote a much fascinated Pedro de Castenada in 1540, first of the Europeans to chronicle the existence of bighorn sheep.

TABLE OF CONTENTS

PREFACE

When early trappers first visited the mountains of the West, they wrote repeatedly about an animal "almost as large as an elk" with magnificent horns that appeared "everywhere." They said the animal was "common," that it was "plentiful," and they left in passing an abundance of names reflecting continuous sightings. This legacy remains, for names such as Sheep Mountain, Sheep Creek, Sheep Butte, Sheep Sheds, and Bighorn Mountain repeatedly appear on maps throughout the West.

So abundant were bighorns that noted trapper Osborn Russell, who traveled the Bighorn Mountains in today's northwestern Wyoming between 1834 and 1843, wrote in his book, *Journal of a Trapper*, that "Thousands of bighorn sheep were scattered up and down feeding on the short grass which grew among the cliffs and crevices; some so high that it required a telescope to see them."

About sheep numbers and great abundance, there can be no question. Renowned naturalist Ernest Thompson Seton estimated in his *Lives of Game Animals* that in a pristine North America, bighorn sheep numbers approached two million. But before the end of the 1800s, the reports began to change, and for obvious reasons. The animal was being hunted to death, even in our early national parks. According to reports, the Bright Angel Trail, which descends into the Grand Canyon of the Colorado River in Arizona, was built on sheep meat. But some of the best documentation comes from Wyoming's Yellowstone, our first national park. In his 1877 report, Superintendent Norris wrote that hide hunters took over 2,000 elk and nearly as many bighorn sheep.

The exploitation of sheep was not confined to the Lower 48, for Dall sheep in Alaska were also hunted relentlessly. Adolf Murie, who pioneered the science of wildlife biology in McKinley (now Denali) National Park, wrote in his classic book, *The Wolves of Mt. McKinley*, about a find he made around 1920: "At an old crumbling cabin on the East Fork River, I found many old ram skulls, most of which were heaped in a pile. There were 142 horns, so at least 71 rams had been brought to this camp. The skulls had been split open, probably to make the brains readily available to the dogs."

Though it is unlikely, mountain sheep might have withstood the ravages of unchecked hunting, but they could not withstand the decimation from diseases settlers brought when they introduced domestic sheep into wild mountain sheep country.

Predictably, the death knell for mountain sheep began to sound: Gone from both North and South Dakota by 1905. Gone from Yosemite National Park by 1914.

And gone from the rugged "breaks" of Montana's Missouri River by 1925; and in this case, the extirpation was particularly tragic, for an entire race, the Audubon bighorn, had been totally eliminated from the face of the earth. In fact, by the turn of the nineteenth century, bighorn sheep numbers dipped to their all-time lows. Decades later, strong conservation practices helped them rebound. But what of them now?

Unfortunately, though sheep numbers have rebounded, populations are once again in a state of flux, for history and prehistory have not been good teachers. In 1996 an entire herd in Idaho's Hells Canyon was devastated by the ravages of a biologic organism that has been reducing wild mountain sheep since Europeans first introduced domestic sheep.

Regrettably, we continue to repeat our mistakes, despite a national referendum by American citizens indicating that on public lands, the needs of wild mountain sheep must come first. Finally, we're hearing the voice of the many—banded now in groups.

What these various groups want to reclaim is an animal that has completed a multitude of narratives that at times approach Homeric proportions—for sheep emerged eons ago in the prehistoric and distant lands of Asia, and then they battled their way to North America. Throughout these great sagas, sheep have exhibited many environmental attainments, some of which I have been privileged to see.

Over the decades, I've trudged throughout the rugged lands that comprise sheep habitat. The first time I saw a band, I remember that in a moment of madness I attempted to follow it for a closer look. But even the lugs on my newly purchased hiking boots were inadequate to maintain balance over the snow, and then out onto the steep rocky slopes over which they galloped. From a considerable distance, I watched as the band moved effortlessly. Before long, a dozen majestic rams crossed the Continental Divide and dropped down into the valley beyond, settling perhaps into some secret crevasse located in this overpowering land of ice and rock, rain and snow, flowers and fog.

In subsequent years, I learned in wildlife management courses more about sheep, for I longed to help the animals prosper. I was not alone.

Today, the dynamics and grandeur of mountain sheep have spawned many extremely enthusiastic supporters. As a result, bighorns once again roam the Black Hills of South Dakota. Amazingly, they now number over 6,700 in Nevada, a state from which they were once extirpated. Certainly, success in restoring sheep has helped create these groups, and today, the hope of preserving bighorns has elevated the animal to a symbol of even greater regional awareness. The bighorn is the symbol of Rocky Mountain National Park; it is the state mammal for both Colorado and Nevada. What's more, there are at least half a dozen organizations dedicated to the proposition that they will restore sheep to their native haunts, where they have always prospered.

Back in their wilderness strong-holds—isolated from man—the great adaptations of mountain sheep provide one of the most successful and far-reaching histories of a wild animal. In part, this is that story, but implicitly, it becomes one of wilderness lost and then partially regained, for to prosper, sheep require remote isolated lands, for mountain sheep are an aloof stately beast—a monarch of the wilds.

In many ways, mountain sheep may be the most imperial of the imperial. I knew that when I first saw them, but to learn of their elaborate social customs, to learn of their incredible odysseys—and all their many other ecological attainments—required many climbs.

Without exceptions, I would repeat them all, for wild mountain sheep swell in the psychic—like tundra swans against the sky, like northern lights sweeping overhead.

They are wild and uninhibited, fighting against a mountain of ice and snow and cold.

Bighorns battle more than any of their cud-chewing brethren.

CHAPTER ONE

SHEEP OF NORTH AMERICA

TERRESTRIAL ECOLOGIST Mark Jorgensen has worked for almost thirty years in Anza Borrego, a state park located in southern California about 50 miles north of Mexico. Because it embraces vast expanses of the Colorado Desert, the Park protects much wilderness as well as herds of peninsular bighorns, a sleek subspecies with clean lines and large horns. During his years in the Park, Jorgensen has tracked, marked, and documented sheep on film. He has presented papers at the prestigious Desert Bighorn Council. He has followed sheep endlessly and knows how elusive they can be even in the desert's vast open spaces. He knows the great distances they can cover, and sometimes he knows why they cover them.

Jorgensen remembers that in 1993 an old ram moved over 70 miles from Borrego Springs, where he first discovered and cared for it. Jorgensen had found the sick ram and placed it in a wild animal park to convalesce. Three weeks later, after a full recovery, he collared the animal and freed it near Montezuma Grade, a Park road that twists through some of the nation's wildest sheep country. At pullouts, interpretative signs along the drive advise you that because sheep blend so well with their surroundings, "You can't see them," but nevertheless, "their eyes are watching you."

Several months after releasing the ram, signals from its transmitter indicated the ram had homed to the rugged, sparsely vegetated desert hills of the San Ysidio Mountains. Then he moved 45 miles to the In-Ko-Pah Mountains, near the Mexican border, where he stayed for a full year until the next summer's breeding season.

"Then," says Jorgensen, "Number 270 disappeared."

Sheep are creatures of the dry, dusty mountainous areas of western North America, thriving along glacial-scoured moraines and the extreme Badlands of South Dakota.

Jorgensen said that to find him, they had to use aircraft. Signals from the collar eventually became strong enough to zero-in on the ram. "Finally," said Jorgensen, "we saw him in the Santa Rosa Mountains." Number 270 had moved 75 miles, and to do so he had to have crossed at least five mountain ranges and three highways to have wound his way through dozens of canyons.

Other biologists relate similar stories. In 1977, over the course of a year, a ram collared in Arizona traveled 43 miles southeast through the Kofa Mountains to the southern Tank Mountains. In Colorado's rugged Rocky Mountain National Park, sheep often move 30 or more miles.

Jorgensen and other biologists emphasize one should not infer sheep always travel such great distances, for they don't. Many sheep never move more than 5 to 10 miles from their place of birth. But every now and then a solitary sheep—or even a band of sheep—decides to wander, and its dispersal into new country has profound biological consequences.

DISPERSAL

Dispersal is biology's release valve, a complex population leveler that reduces inbreeding and allows reinvasion of old haunts. In some cases it prods animals into lands never before occupied. Over a period of, say, a

On average, the horns of desert bighorn ewes are larger than those of their more northern counterparts. The lack of available water holes requires them to fight more.

million years, dispersal can be substantial.

Sheep didn't originate in North America. Nor, for that matter, did a host of other species that we consider native. Moose didn't, nor did the deer or goat. Sheep, however, were among the forerunners.

Valerius Geist, perhaps North America's most recognized expert on sheep, in his book, *Mountain Sheep: A Study in Behavior and Evolution*, wrote, "By being able to live on dry, dusty plants, sheep can exploit a reserve of poor forage and thrive where many other herbivores cannot." Because sheep have a digestive system unlike any other ruminant, that is precisely what they did. As the massive ice sheets receded, sheep in Asia advanced, eating and thriving on the dusty, mud-covered plants that emerged in the wake of glaciers.

Sheep, of course, were unaware that they were paving a route; they simply followed their instinctive urge to disperse, perhaps because of overcrowding. Or perhaps because one or two in the group were lovesick, like Number 270 may have been.

THE ARC OF WILD MOUNTAIN SHEEP

Whatever the reason or reasons—through moves that sometimes may have been motivated by the desire to procreate—sheep eventually came to inhabit a broad arc. That arc sweeps from Asia across the Bering Strait, down the mountain ranges of Alaska and Canada southward to the western portion of the United States, and eventually into the mountains of Mexico's Baja California and Sonora.

In the northern part of the American arc, sheep occupy the Brooks and Alaska ranges. In Canada, they occupy the Rockies, while in the Lower 48 the arc embraces the Rockies and the Sierra Nevadas, as well as many outliers. Sheep in these areas, particularly those in the Rockies, tend to occupy the lee side of a mountain's prevailing weather pattern, where moisture deposits are less. In the West, typically these "rain shadows" are confined to a mountain's east-facing slopes, where vegetation is sparse and vision is usually maximized.

Forty races live in this 8,000-mile-long swath. Of those races, ten existed during pristine times in North America. Nine of those races still live, inhabiting such diverse areas as highlighted by the parched wastelands of Death Valley. There, sheep learned to cope not only with temperatures that soar to over 130°F but with other hardships associated with arid country. In deserts, they confronted water scarcity and the sharp agave thorns that penetrate the skin to rake the bone.

Overleaf: Most horn growth begins in the summer and continues until the fall rut when sex hormones turn on, leaving the dark growthless "age ring."

In some parts of their vast intercontinental arc, sheep once ventured to elevations above 20,000 feet and could do so in North America if required. Historically, they were abundant near the 14,110-foot-high tip of Colorado's Pike's Peak and on California's Sierra Nevadas and White Mountains. They still thrive along the snow- and wind-battered slopes of Alaska's Denali National Park, where they cope with temperatures that dip to minus 70°F.

The arc of sheep country also includes the jumbled landscapes of Arches and Canyonlands national parks, the steep cliffs of the Grand Canyon as well as a multitude of other land forms such as those in Glacier and Yellowstone; and those, too, in Canada's Kluane, Jasper, Banff, and Yoho national parks. Indeed, sheep epitomize the definition of success, for among wild mammals, only a few—such as the grizzly bear, coyote, and skunk—equal the sheep's ability to adapt to such immense and varied landscapes.

EVOLUTION

Mountain sheep evolved from a stock known as the *Rupicaprini*, a biological group that also includes goats, the closest relative of sheep. Because the fossil record is scarce, biologists question which specific ancestor gave rise to sheep. Records only permit a distant link with the common ancestor of both goats and sheep.

Whatever the precise origin, the distant ancestor of modern sheep began responding to an urge to move during the early Pleistocene, a geological time period that began about 2 million years ago. The period was an epoch of some of the world's greatest climatic change, and sheep and other species responded with bewildering changes of their own. Fossil remains from that time include gigantic deer and moose, whose horns and antlers were twice those of modern-day species. Among sheep, there were giants weighing up to 450 pounds. There were also dwarfs, such as the Cyprus urials, which seldom topped 80 pounds.

But the land worked its magic and, eventually, a sheep evolved that we may consider to have been today's predecessor. Perhaps it was this sheep that chanced upon the mountains flanking the Bering Sea and also

Ancestors of our mountain sheep (such as this desert bighorn) departed Asia almost 2 million years ago. They reached North America about 1 million years ago where they evolved into nine still-existing subspecies.

confronted Beringia (the Bering Land Bridge)—that ancient mysterious stretch of land that from time to time has permitted the intermingling of plants and animals between two vastly different continents.

BATTLE OF BERINGIA

Two million years ago, ice began to choke the mainland areas of North America and northern Asia, binding the seas that withdrew from the shallows between modern-day Russia and the United States. Over the eons, on at least four different occasions, a land bridge slowly emerged from the misty surface of the Bering Sea that connected the two continental shores. When the world warmed, a shallow ocean covered the land between Siberia and Alaska. When it cooled, vast ice sheets spread outward from the polar regions. It was then that sea levels dropped, falling as much as 300 or 400 feet. Across this land bridge, sometimes shrouded by fog, whipped often by winds and heavy seas, pounded the distant relatives of today's mountain sheep.

By no means did these early pioneers have the country to themselves. At the same time sheep battled their way across Beringia, other species also advanced, among them the forerunners of the moose, elk, musk-oxen, bison, and goats. In turn, they met a gauntlet of predators that had already made their way across this 50-mile-long bridge of land. This array included the predecessor of the black bear, wolf, coyote, and wolverine.

Upon reaching the mainland, sheep entered an ice-free northwestern Alaska. Some must ultimately have returned in the opposite direction. But many more followed the melting ice sheets south, exploring new terrain, eventually coming to populate all areas for which their biology was appropriate.

Throughout these vast periods of migration, geologists say that the land of northwestern Alaska remained ice-free, separated for lengthy periods from lands to the south by the same massive ice sheets that opened Beringia. The presence of these ice masses led to the differences between the two major groupings of sheep now wandering North America.

BIGHORNS AND THINHORNS

Scientists group North American sheep on the basis of their horns, for they believe the horn types evolved under different circumstances created by geological separation. In general, Canada's Peace River Valley provides a boundary. Those found to the north are called thinhorns, while those to the south are called bighorns.

Glaciers created the two major evolving groupings by initially separating them by both time and space. Sheep of the big-horned variety were the first to migrate across Beringia, perhaps a million years ago. When the weather warmed, melting the glaciers that had barricaded movements, these populations dispersed south, for once again Beringia was inundated and those inclined to disperse had no other choice. When the weather cooled, subsequent glaciers choked their lands now to the north, isolating these first groups of travelers from bands that later crossed Beringia, for now they were blocked.

Ten thousand years ago, a final group migrated across Beringia, mixing with those that had not dispersed southward. They, too, were confined to this ice-free refuge in northwestern Alaska, for once again their movements south were deterred by glaciation. Here they remained—and evolved—where they became thinhorns.

Species within Species

With the two major species widely separated and free to develop independently in large ice-free areas, yet other varieties evolved, for climatic conditions are ever in a state of flux. We know the geography of North America has changed, and are often reminded in dramatic ways, as when

Mountain sheep are grouped into two major divisions that include both the bighorns and thinhorns, such as this Stone sheep.

Mount Saint Helens erupted in 1980; or when we drive past Canada's mighty Athabascan Glacier, now receding. Likewise, populations within the two major groupings became separated by floods, earthquakes, and other forces still acting today. Because of these separations, eight subspecies arose within the big-horned populations. The list includes the now-extinct Audubon bighorn, Rocky Mountain bighorn, the California bighorn, and four races collectively called desert bighorns. Of these, the Rocky Mountain bighorn is the largest, most abundant, and the most northern in range.

In a similar fashion, three subspecies arose from the thin-horned sheep, the Dall, the Stone, and the Kenai Peninsula Dall sheep. Today, nine different subspecies of mountain sheep, both thin-horned and big-horned, roam throughout North America. Biologists can detect these differences macroscopically and, quite significantly, microscopically. On the molecular level, the sophisticated technique of chromosome mapping shows much chemical and cellular variation.

On the macroscopic level, the obvious difference is in their horns. Though there are overlaps—and therefore there can be no hard-and-fast division on the basis of horn size—thin-horned sheep have horns that average 12½ inches at the base. Big-horned sheep have horns that measure up to 17 inches at the base.

Despite the variations, the differences are not sufficient to prevent one subspecies from breeding with another. In the wild, cross-breeding usually doesn't happen. But just as wolves, coyotes, and dogs can interbreed, mating among various sheep can also occur. Social pressures help maintain the integrity of these species and subspecies, and do create some order, but mating naturally occurs among the various subspecies.

POWER OF THE LAND

Wild country can also shape mountain sheep. Jeff Grandison, a wildlife program coordinator in Cedar City, Utah, who has worked extensively with wild sheep, says that he has taken desert bighorns and placed them in country once inhabited by Rocky Mountain bighorns. Within a few years, the desert bighorns had all the characteristics of the Rocky Mountain bighorns. "The point," says Grandison, "is that the country shapes the sheep."

In Baja, California, sheep are leggier, finer, and smaller muscled than sheep in the more northern habitat of Montana, Wyoming, Colorado, and Canada.

To survive with predators, mountain sheep such as these Dall sheep prefer the high open country that maximizes their superior eyesight.

Weights are also indicative of habitat. A 10-year-old sheep in Montana and southern Alberta will average 285 pounds, while a mature desert bighorn will average only 191. Ewes in these same respective groups average 136 and 115 pounds.

Structurally, the various races of desert bighorns have longer tooth rows and broader noses than the Rocky Mountain races. Ears in desert bighorns are longer, to help disperse heat. The color of hides differs too. In desert forms, coats are usually paler, but only after the sun has had a chance to bleach out the hair.

Some may say that if these differences are only superficial, why complicate things with detailed groupings? Jim DeForge, Director of the Bighorn Institute in Palm Desert, California, says that if nothing else, grouping maintains a geographical integrity, facilitating management.

LIMITING FACTORS

In the wild, sheep require open country where they can optimize the use of their superb vision. They must also have access to good lambing areas. But, perhaps the most significant "limiting factor" against sheep further expanding their ranges is found in the species' need for escape terrain. Escape terrain is the Achilles' heel of mountain sheep; it confines them to the immense arc they now occupy in the mountains and prevents them from crossing the featureless expanse found within the Great Plains. In the same way that marshes limit the snail darter, the prairie limits the antelope, and forests limit the black bear, so escape terrain has limited the eastward expansion of bighorn sheep. If wild mountain sheep can't escape predators, obviously their expansion is checked.

END OF THE LINE

When Number 270 was tagged, he was an 8-year-old animal. When he died, he was a ram that had lived to the ripe old age of 10. Jorgensen said that in his prime, 270 was a magnificent animal. During his wild, wandering days, 270 undoubtedly sired many offspring, perhaps as many as 30 lambs, which in turn, gave rise to other offspring. And that is his legacy—a rich and diverse flow of genetic material now dispersed over as many as five different mountain ranges.

Periodically, sheep are forced to water holes, placing them in harm's way, for predators are many.

Overleaf: The Badlands of South Dakota mark the species' eastward extension. The Audubon bighorn once roamed these lands, but the last one was killed at Magpie Creek, North Dakota, in 1905.

CHAPTER TWO

IT'S ALL PHYSICAL

THE ABILITY OF AN ANIMAL TO ADAPT to its surroundings determines whether a species will survive. In the case of mountain sheep, all of the various races adapted well to an environment that for much of the time was always just in front of advancing glaciers. In fact, everything about sheep says that the species has acclimated to a rugged environment, and that it has done so from horns to hooves.

HORNS

Bighorn sheep have always moved people to exaggerate, and for a number of years the overstatements persisted. Many stern-faced accounts appeared in print as recently as the late 1800s, proclaiming that stampeded sheep would launch themselves from the highest cliffs, fall on their horns and then arise, uninjured.

Though bighorn sheep have massive horns rooted firmly to solid skulls, horns do have limitations. But it is easy to understand the considerable confusion, attendant myths, and misinformed interpretations.

Horn growth begins from a bony core. Around the core of bone, keratin—a material that resembles human fingernails and that is found in hooves and constitutes the actual horn—begins to envelop the bone. Over several years, the keratin soon completely covers and extends beyond the bony core. The bony core ensures growth, for as the years progress, the core develops a multitude of honeycombed chambers that provide avenues for blood vessels and nerves. In turn, the vessels and nerves support, maintain, and provide the physiological mechanism for additional horn growth.

Subject of awe since first seen by Spanish conquistadors,
bighorn sheep and their horns have generated many myths.

Both males and females grow horns, and up to about the age of 18 months, growth is similar. But when the horns of females reach 12 to 18 inches, horn growth then stops, while that of young rams continues. Contrasting an 18-month-old yearling with an 8- to 9-year-old ram shows an increased body weight of $1\frac{3}{4}$ times. But by comparison, the horns of an older ram have increased their length about 4 times, and their horn circumference about $2\frac{1}{2}$ times. Horn weight, however, has soared from about $1\frac{1}{2}$ pounds to over 30 pounds, an increase of 24 times. Eventually the weight of skull and horns will equal that of the animal's entire skeleton, or as much as $\frac{1}{10}$ of the ram's total weight.

Huge horns are the normal state of affairs. Unlike the antlers of elk, moose, and deer, which are shed annually, the horns of mountain sheep are retained throughout their lives. Here is where rams record their battles, their good and bad years. Here a ram records his age. Not surprisingly, much of a ram's stature within the herd is determined by his genetic capacity to produce large horns.

According to Nevada biologist Craig Stevenson, horn growth is dependent on a variety of factors, including diet. Throughout life, horn development depends on the mineral content of the soil, and researchers well know that the limestone areas in Glacier National Park north through Canada's Waterton National Park produce sheep with some of North America's largest horns.

One particularly magnificent ram had a horn length of 41 inches, with a circumference of $17\frac{1}{4}$ inches and a tip-to-tip measurement of 26 inches. Other rams have produced larger horns, but with smaller bases. One had a right horn that measured $49\frac{1}{2}$ inches, the left $48\frac{1}{4}$ inches. Stone sheep, Dall sheep, and desert bighorns have all, at one time or another, produced horns that approach these records held by bighorn rams.

GROWTH RINGS

Because horns are never dropped and because of a peculiarity unique to sheep, their horns can chronicle age. Stevenson, who teaches an indoctrination course on sheep for the state of Nevada, says rams generally add a growth ring each time they come into the rut. During this period, rams produce testosterone, a male hormone. So much of their time goes into breeding that food and the resulting energy levels are inadequate to both fuel the body and sustain horn growth. At that time, horn growth

Overleaf: Horns of this four-year-old ram may eventually comprise over 13 percent of its body weight.

slows and the cells in the horns darken, producing the characteristic growth rings used to age them.

Much the same happens to ewes, but their glands produce estrogen. The results are similar, though not nearly so dramatic.

Stevenson says that anyone with patience and a good spotting scope can determine the age of mountain sheep. In his lectures, Stevenson emphasizes the idiosyncrasies as well as the consistencies in the rings. Six-year-old rams produce horns that inscribe three-quarters (generally) of a circle. Not until eight bands inscribe their horns will a ram (generally) reach full-curl designation. With some practice, Stevenson says you can almost pinpoint a ram's age, though you must understand the biology of horns and recognize its limitations.

The annual growth ring is not obvious the first year, though it is produced. The ring is an indistinct ripple along the side of the horn. Rams 2 years old usually lay down a pair of bands, indicating they are growing up. By the third year, young rams have matured, at least sexually. "He's in his teenage years," says Stevenson, "and sometimes the hormones race, sometimes withdraw." Growth rings reflect that this pattern for energy is shunted.

Rams wear their autobiographies on their horns. Rings tell age, brooming attempts to improve vision, and gouges and brooming reveal past battles.

Sometimes energy is available for horn growth, but often much of it goes into the demands imposed by the rut. These rams can lay down as many as four or five tightly spaced bands, which together make one thick ring.

At age 4, rams are ready to procreate and testosterone levels rise. Among desert bighorns, hormone production continues throughout the summer. In the North, production starts in September and slows in December.

Among 4-year-old rams the band is dark and continuous, and is generally the first deep, dark, solid band that completely encircles the horn.

Horns never stop growing, but from 8 years on, rings grow much closer, particularly toward the base where growth occurs. Rams also

A variety of factors, including weather, influence the annual growth rate of horns.

"broom," or blunt, their horns by rubbing the tips against rocks and trees. The effect is to produce square tips and eliminate evidence of the first year's growth, which is at the tip. Seldom, if ever, do sheep permit their horns to obscure their vision, something that might happen if rams did not cut them back by brooming.

By the end of the second year, some rams may have broomed over 50 percent of the first year's growth, while ewes may have broomed only 30 percent. By 10 to 12 years of age, rams have broomed over 95 percent of their first year's horn growth. In rams that survive past age 13, horn growth may be minuscule. In older individuals, brooming sometimes exceeds growth, meaning horns can actually get smaller.

Horn growth and annual ring development may slow for other reasons. Sometimes in the North, so much energy has gone into breeding that winter horn growth—and the complementary ring—slows. Much the same occurs in the desert, where water is a critical factor. When water is scarce, rams lack the energy to both fuel their bodies and grow horns. In some rare cases—because there was no opportunity for growth throughout the entire year—bighorns may not develop a ring at all.

HORN PRINTS

In a classic desert study conducted by biologists Ralph and Florence Welles in 1952, the couple listed 51 individual sheep they could identify by "horn prints." Like fingerprints, no two horns are alike. In their cast of characters, the team named sheep by the tightness of the curl, the spread of horns and the degree of brooming. They evaluated the chips, nicks, breaks, and the degree of ridging. If these features were prominent, they named the animal. In so doing, they could identify an animal as surely as if they dabbed its body with paint, encircled its neck with a collar, or attached an aluminum tag to its ear. Dr. Jerry Freilich, an ecologist stationed in Joshua Tree National Park in the mid-1990s, so thoroughly believed in the technique that he has used it in his own research efforts. "It works," say Freilich, "and we're telling staff members that when they see sheep, they should look for chips, breaks, or anything else that might stand out." Freilich emphasizes they also look for other distinguishing features, such as the rump patch, which varies from individual to individual.

Some of the features that helped Welles and Welles distinguish individuals have been tabulated, as such characteristics continue to occur.

BODY AND SENSES

Although horns distinguish mountain sheep, many other features help them adapt to the country in which they live. Ernest Thompson Seton

"With apparent unconcern," wrote Captain Meriwether Lewis, bighorn sheep cross a cliff face in places where "had they made one false step the[y] must have precipitated" to their death.

noted these qualities when he quoted an Indian guide as saying, "Bighorns can't hear thunder, can't smell dead horse, but can see through rock."

Sheep see well, as the old guide realized. That's the reason sheep seek terrain that is unobstructed by trees; they want to be able to see long distances so they have ample time to evade their predators. Just how well bighorns see is subject to some speculation. Several naturalists have said that sheep have the equivalent of an 8-power set of binoculars, and noted sheep hunter and author Jack O'Connor said he concurred. He based his belief on his observation of a ram that was watching a coyote that he could not see with his naked eye, but could see with an 8x30 set of binoculars. O'Connor said, however, that many biologists are reluctant to commit themselves on the issue of sight. He also wrote that although the eyes of sheep are good, they are inferior to those of a pronghorn antelope.

Despite the lack of resolution of the question, what cannot be disputed is that sheep do have excellent vision, and that they maximize this capability. When lounging in a group, sheep lie at different angles so that every conceivable direction of approach is covered. In this way they further protect themselves through their "many eyes."

Sheep undoubtedly also have good senses of smell and hearing, but in the mountains these traits are less important than is the sense of sight. In the mountains, wind currents are erratic, rendering less important the sense of smell. As well, the sense of hearing is nowhere near as important in rocky, mountainous areas where there are but few twigs and branches to broadcast a predator's approach. What is important, therefore, is excellent vision and a body built to move quickly in the environment in which it has evolved.

Bighorns are compact, and at maturity, large males can weigh 300 pounds, though there is much regional variation, as reflected by the writings of early-day adventurers. Audubon, the famous naturalist of the mid 1800s, after whom the Audubon sheep was named, tells of a badlands bighorn that weighed 344 pounds. And in 1920, Ernest Thompson Seton, a man noted for his keen observations, wrote in his *Lives of Game Animals* that sheep averaged 300 pounds.

Though large mule deer weigh about the same as bighorns, sheep are proportioned differently. Sheep are more chunky, particularly in the front quarter, which is layered with muscle needed for leaping among the broken country they prefer. Sheep are shorter of leg, which tends to reduce the amount of exposed surface area—a cold-weather adaptation.

In North America the only hooved animal with which sheep might be confused is the mountain goat. However, in national parks within the Lower 48, sheep and goats only occur together naturally in Montana's Glacier National Park, where their ranges overlap. Sheep and goats are also found together in South Dakota's Custer State Park—in 1924 goats escaped into the Park from a zoo which the park managed. Today there are about 170 goats in the Black Hills.

In Canada's national parks, goats and sheep are found together in many mountain ranges. Once in Jasper, Alberta, I saw a herd of sheep gathering at a salt lick. After their departure, a band of goats scampered in. Usually goats and sheep keep their distance, each seeking its own preferred habitat.

The most obvious means of differentiating the two species is by their horns, particularly those of males. On bighorns, tan growths begin at a broad base and then arc back, terminating in a point that is usually blunt. In goats, black horns project dangerously upward, terminating in a point.

Where ranges overlap, as in Canada, the sheep's grayish body coat distinguishes it from the goat's pure white. But in the extreme North, the coat of Dall sheep is as white as freshly fallen snow. Not to worry, for here the ranges of the two don't overlap.

Invariably, there are no hard-and-fast rules for distinguishing between the two. Dick Coe, a naturalist in Colorado's Rocky Mountain National Park, reports that in the spring, "sheep in the Mummy Range herd have a yellow-white coat, due to the sun at the higher altitudes bleaching their coats." Coe says sheep in the Cow Creek herd have the typical gray-brown coat because they "winter lower, at about 8,000 to 9,000 feet." Coe says that many people, upon seeing ewes in the Mummy Range herd, believe they are seeing goats.

Nevertheless, in their more southern reaches, bighorns do tend to be brown or some lighter variation thereof. Surprisingly, in their more northern range, where there is more snow and it would appear white might offer some survival benefits for camouflage, bighorns are an even darker brown, some believe for heat retention.

Bighorn sheep—and the thin-horned Stone sheep—all have a lightly colored rump patch that is distinctly set off from the dark fur of the body. The tails of both are broad and dark. In Dall sheep, the tail is simply a continuation of the animal's snow-white body.

SUITING UP FOR THE COLD

Few species have adapted to a more rugged set of conditions than have the mountain sheep of North America. One October several years ago, my wife and I learned just how successful they were. During the night, the skies had cleared and the temperature plummeted. My thermometer appeared stuck at minus 13°F.

A compact, blocky stature and millions of hollow hairs help sheep retain body heat.

Leaving behind the relative comforts (icicles formed from our breath, clinging to the vehicle's interior) of our camper van, we hiked on the surrounding hills located in Alberta's Banff National Park. We were looking for sheep, which we had glimpsed the previous day along the slopes flanking the Bow River. What, we wondered, but the most self-assured animal would choose to live in extremes such as these? But scattered before us were rams, ewes, and lambs, most with crusted snow clinging to their hides and clumping around their eyes. And all around them were depressions in the snow, heralding that they had weathered a frigid night, out in the open in the howling wind.

Jane and I walked over to the depressions and gathered snow from their beds. The snow was slightly crusted, indicating that little heat had escaped from the bodies of these superbly insulated animals.

While it is true that goats may have a very slight edge on cold-weather adaptations, sheep don't trail far behind. On a scale of 1 to 10 for adapting to cold weather, we concluded that sheep register 9.5. But for overall adaptability in our hypothetical system of measure, they rate a 10. Only the grizzly bear matches the sheep for its range of tolerances, though in the winter, it cheats by hibernating. Not so the sheep. Goats on the other hand sometimes enter caves in the winter, where they sink into a state of intense lethargy.

Sheep are wonderfully shaped for cold-weather survival. Though their legs are trim, there is nothing fragile about them.

Overleaf: Winter triggers many physiological adaptations that diminish the season's harshness.

Their thick shoulders present a compact, blocky appearance that serves to conserve heat. By comparison, goats appear more delicate.

In contrast to mule deer—the other species that sometimes encroaches on sheep terrain—bighorns are relatively short-legged. Though slightly disproportionate in appearance, this harmony of trunk and limbs reduces the amount of exposed surface area, further diminishing heat loss from radiation. Heat that does escape from their bodies is held tightly by millions of hollow hairs. Goats, in turn, neatly trap body heat with a combination of long hairs overlying mats of wool.

Sheep also confront the cold through physiological adaptations,

If food is scarce, the circulatory system can shut down, allowing sheep to conserve energy and diminish their need for food.

particularly important for those members living in high, cold country. At higher altitudes, the heart must pump harder and expend more energy to compensate for lack of oxygen. At such times, the metabolic rate goes up and the animal requires more fuel. In winter, when food is scarce, the circulatory system can almost shut down, placing sheep in a "survival" mode, which allows them to conserve energy and drastically decrease their need for food.

STRIPPING DOWN FOR SUMMER

Sheep have adapted not only to the cold, but to the heat, by both panting and sweating. In the desert, sheep actively seek overhangs and caves,

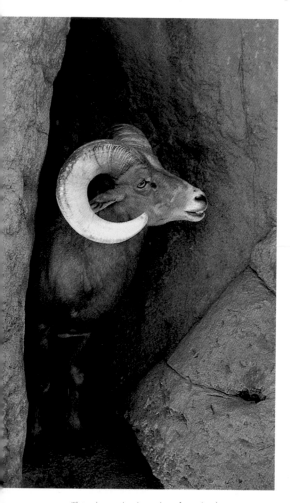

where they remain inactive during the hottest part of the day. Sheep also use caves for other reasons, and old-timers in Montana named an entire mountain face "Sheep Sheds," because sheep made continuous use of the area's many caverns. They, too, want reprieve from the elements, different though they may be from conditions found in the desert.

In the 1920s, Vernon Bailey, one of the first scientists to work for the U.S. Biological Survey, wrote that sheep have used New Mexico's Carlsbad Caves through the ages as a refuge from storms, and that they have used the springs in the cave as a source of water. Sheep, according to Bailey, also used the caves for protection from predators, apparently feeling no entrapment.

"Bear tracks," wrote Bailey, "are sometimes found in the cave, but the mountain sheep would have a fair chance to escape from bears or mountain lions, as the cave is wide and clear . . ."

This desert bighorn has found refuge from the elements in a cave.

Though sheep maximize the environment to their advantage, their biology plays the biggest role in their adaptability, for sheep create their own shelter in terms of their coats and then shed much of that "shelter" in accordance with where they live. In the South, sheep shed early, often as early as March. Sheep in the North molt in the summer months, usually in June. In Alaska, they shed and then begin to regrow coats of hair almost immediately.

Molting is a dramatic event. Hair comes off in mats, draping from the animal like so many towels. The process is often associated with some discomfort, for during such periods, sheep search for trees and rocky cliffs to serve as scratching boards. In Glacier National Park, I have seen stunted trees in alpine areas covered with modest-sized rugs of hair.

About one month is required to shed the winter coat, though this may vary, particularly among animals that are sick or run down. Sick animals often retain their coats throughout the summer, then shed them almost overnight. Author Charles Hansen wrote in *The Desert Bighorn* that "This information about shedding can give some idea as to the number of sick animals in the herd and as to the age and condition of the ewes." In healthy animals, molting normally progresses from the belly and rump upward and forward. The hair around the chest and upper portions of their backs is retained longest.

Shortly after shedding, sheep begin growing their coats anew. Somewhere between September and early October, they have grown back a dark coat, which in bighorns is mottled by patches of light fur. When they

Molting is a perfectly normal event, but the manner in which sheep shed provides an indication of individual health.

reach their fall rutting grounds, these spots will have turned dark and their coats will be uniform, except for their faces and for the light rump patch.

FOOTWEAR

Mountain sheep live in environments dangerous to many mammals. To survive, nature has provided them with a number of features that help them go where few others can. Sheep have made the mountains their domain, leaping and cavorting in the roughest of country. To do so, sheep have developed feet that are almost skid-proof, something that must be seen to be appreciated.

In Banff National Park, Jane and I once followed a small herd to a point where literally thousands of sheep tracks coursed up and through the rocks. Some followed a straight line, some followed a somewhat sinuous line, while others had absolutely no imaginable pattern at all. What these tracks shared in common was their sure-footed appearance. Elongated skid marks were few, and what few there were remained true to a direct course. Not so with our own tracks, which sometimes skidded and careened wildly.

Sheep negotiate the terrain with remarkable agility, traveling along the level at speeds of up to 30 miles per hour. Even when they climb, they cover in minutes terrain that a person would need hours to ascend. Mountain sheep accomplish these feats in part because they have squarish hooves shaped to grip surfaces. Montana Biologist Kim Keating has said the hooves of sheep are like tennis shoes but with a hard core ringing skid-proof soles. He emphasizes that they are not suction cups.

Vernon Bailey, in his early studies, wrote that he was struck first of all by the differences between the front and hind feet. "The front being fully twice as large as the hind, much squarer in form, with deeper, heavier cushioned heels, and lighter less-worn dew claws." The renowned biologist went on to say that the greater wear of the hind dew claws is easily accounted for by their constant use in holding back as the sheep goes downhill. "It is easy to see," wrote Bailey, "how they [the hooves] would fit and cling to the smooth surface of a sloping rock where wholly hard hooves like those of a horse would slip, just as you can turn your back to a steep slope of glacier-polished granite and walk up it on the palms of your hands where you can not take one step with the roughest of hobnailed shoes."

As June Sampson, Director of the Bighorn Sheep Center in Wyoming, told me, "The hooves of sheep are shaped to splay." By that, she implied that sheep can move forward—and do so rapidly—through country so treacherous that other species, if they were to follow, would undoubtedly perish.

Sheep like this Dall negotiate rugged terrain with hooves that bear some resemblance to tennis shoes.

Overleaf: Even the young can negotiate treacherous country.

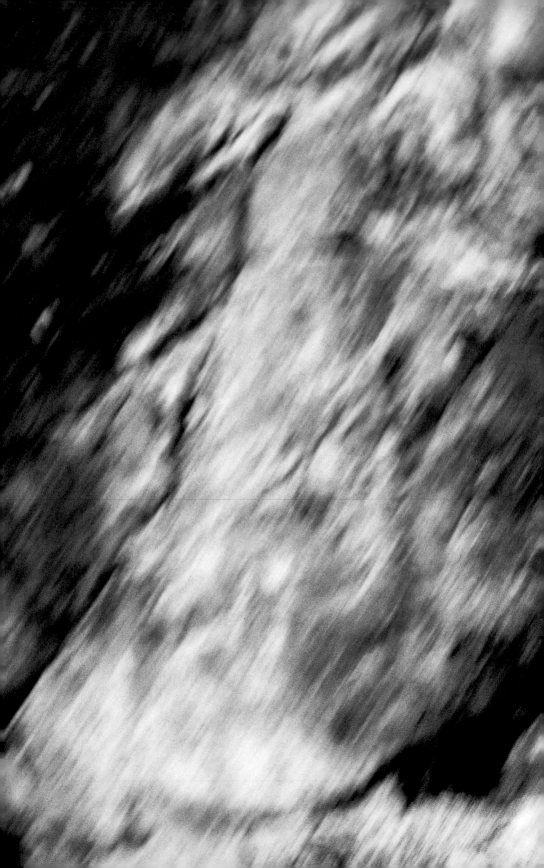

CHAPTER THREE

A Pyramid of Life

GREEN PLANTS are considered "producers" because of their unique ability to capture light energy from the sun and use it to transform carbon dioxide and water into food. Animals that feed on these plants—called "consumers"—that are in turn fed upon by other more powerful animals can all be considered part of a large community. Within this community, there are primary consumers that feed on vegetation, secondary consumers preying on primary consumers, and tertiary consumers, such as the grizzly, that feed on both producers and consumers.

In general, biologists categorize mountain sheep as primary consumers, but at times, sheep exhibit such diverse feeding habits that some refer to them in a casual way as opportunistic, for it seems they can eat most anything. More commonly, however, mountain sheep must evade a number of secondary consumers, which, in the prime of their lives, they do with extraordinary agility. As with all other forms of life, time eventually takes its toll, and that's when the various demands of life begin to exert themselves.

Biologists classify *Ovus*, as "primary consumers," because they are among the first to convert the energy in grass to usable food.

FOOD OPTIONS

Of the various terms that might be used to describe the feeding habits of sheep, perhaps the most appropriate is "opportunistic." Biologists have watched sheep stand on their hind legs, front legs stretched high for bracing, to take the flowering parts of a Joshua tree. They've seen them eat the dried stalks of the yucca plant and strip away the bark of trees. In one rare instance, when Biologist Kim Keating was working in Yellowstone National Park on the Mount Everts winter range, he watched an adult female "consume" a bone from a small ungulate (hooved mammal) in about 5 to 10 minutes. Keating said the bone was probably from a bighorn sheep, mule deer, or pronghorn antelope.

In Texas, Burch Carson, a biologist employed in 1941 by the Texas Game Fish and Oyster Commission, believed that bighorns browse on most everything that grows in the mountains. "When a complete list of all the desert bighorn's food is compiled," wrote Carson, "it will be very long." Included in Carson's baseline list were Spanish dagger blossoms and, in the fall, dagger apples, which Carson termed the bighorn's "candy."

Sheep feed in a variety of conditions. During the winter, some of the most severe are found in Yellowstone National Park. There, sheep paw through deep snow for food.

More recent studies have not shortened Carson's long list, though sheep do have regional preferences. In the Northwest, sheep eat many things but prefer grasses. When grasses are not available, they shift to the buds of aspen, spruce, Douglas fir, willow, currant, rose, and juniper. In the Southwest, though they prefer grasses, they also live on shrubs such as mountain mahogany, Mormon tea, and buckbrush.

Sheep can digest many forms of food, and their teeth form the foundation for this tolerance. Like other hoofed animals, they begin life with milk teeth which, in sheep, are replaced by permanent teeth no later than age 4. The lower incisors and single canine are intended for nipping while the molars serve to grind. Between the molars and the incisors is a wide space or "diastema." Behind each diastema is a single row of molars, which, because of great wear from grinding coarse food, grow throughout life.

Sheep have a four-chambered stomach, as do other cud chewers. But that's where one of the biggest differences between them lies. In sheep, the first stomach—called the rumen—is unusually large, creating a super fermentation vat. More than any other feature, it was the enlarged rumen that enabled sheep to live at the edge of glaciers, to digest dry, dusty greenery, and to colonize two continents.

The cud—a wad of hastily swallowed food—travels back up the gullet for a thorough chewing. After chewing, the food is swallowed again, where it moves quickly through the rumen and on to the three other stomachs for digestion.

Though sheep are capable of grazing widely, the nutritional value of food is really quite important, particularly in colder climates. In the North, frigid conditions extract a higher metabolic price and sheep must eat more high-energy foods than their southern counterparts.

Wherever they live, mountain sheep average several pounds of dry greenery apiece each day. In the high country of Wyoming's Wind River Mountains, 500 to 1,200 square feet of land are needed to produce the 4 pounds of vegetation a sheep eats every day. In an average winter, it needs 150 times that amount. If the food supply is reduced, the number of sheep the area can support is also reduced. In the vernacular of the biologist, this is called the land's "carrying capacity." To be effective, range managers must thoroughly understand these complex ecological interactions of wildlife with the land.

If there are more animals in the area than it can support, the extra animals will not survive. The added pressure of too many sheep results in long-lasting harmful effects on the rangeland. Overused rangeland also drives sheep to marginal areas, where they succumb to predation. Likewise, when water is limited, sheep tire and must look to unfamiliar territory, both exposing and expending themselves.

Overleaf: In the high country, typically 500 to 1,200 square feet of land are needed to produce the 4 pounds of vegetation sheep such as this Dall eat every day.

Miracle at the Spring

In addition to food, sheep, of course, have other essential needs which, if lacking, can spell disaster. In the North, sheep can usually eat snow to replenish water losses. Not so in the desert. Here sheep frequently go days and even weeks without water. To get by, sheep eat the water-holding leaves of the barrel cactus. But eventually, sheep must have free water. Without it, ewes often abandon lambs; and sometimes mating is postponed—or forgotten. Without water, sheep eventually die one way or another.

On more than one occasion Welles and Welles—renowned Death Valley researchers—wrote they had watched two sheep drink deeply from springs when temperatures hovered at 113°F in the shade. Water produced such profound results that the researchers called the transformation the "Miracle at the Springs."

". . . I was marveling," wrote Welles, "at how two animals in such poor condition could do this when I suddenly realized that they were no longer in poor condition! The potbellies were gone, the legs were no longer spindly, and the muscles were smooth and rounded beneath the glistening hides of animals in perfect health. This rapid recovery from it [dehydration], this complete rehydration in so short a time seemed little short of miraculous when observed in full context and relatively. It is one of the most significant single observations we have made."

Death Valley bighorns need water year-round, drinking every 3 to 5 days. Frequently, Welles and Welles watched as sheep drank measured quantities from a tank. One ram drank 7 gallons, increasing its weight by 23 percent. On another occasion a ewe and a ram lamb drank an estimated 20 percent of their body weight. Many guzzled as much as 1 gallon per minute.

By comparison, camels can typically lose 25 percent of their body weight without serious consequences. When humans lose 12 percent of their body weight from dehydration, they die.

When nutritional requirements aren't met, sheep tire more readily, becoming more susceptible to predation, and are unable to ward off the debilitating effects of parasites.

When water is available, sheep can rehydrate themselves almost instantly from losses that can approach as much as 20 percent.

THE PREDATOR EQUATION

Dick Coe has a fascination for sheep that is derived from a labor of love. Coe was a naturalist at Rocky Mountain National Park in the 1990s and has made sheep his area of specialization, observing them at every available opportunity. Coe has watched sheep and coyotes interact. He's seen sheep elude coyotes. He's also seen coyotes take sheep and knows the circumstances under which coyotes are most successful.

From mid-May to mid-July, ewes bring their lambs down from Bighorn Mountain to the mineral lick at Sheep Lake. The mineral lick is high in many essential elements, such as sodium and magnesium. Lactating ewes must have sufficient mineral content to maintain the quality of the milk supply. Often, the demands of their bodies drive them to the licks.

For centuries sheep have been congregating at the lick. So have coyotes, but for much different reasons, and Coe remembers one incident.

"Seven ewes brought seven lambs to the lick," said Coe. "All of a sudden a coyote appeared, separating a lamb from a ewe, running it back and forth. Within seconds it had blooded the lamb's hindquarters, weakening the animal."

Several hours later, Coe found the remains of the lamb in a brush pile. "It was gutted," recalls Coe of the incident, giving the appearance that more than one animal had feasted well. "It's part of the balance of nature," says Coe, who is not an apologist for coyotes, realizing that populations of sheep—just like those of starlings, Australian rabbits, and locusts—must be in balance. In this way, sheep also fulfill a complex function in the pyramid of life. As animals that eat vegetation, sheep are classified by biologists as primary consumers, serving as a food base for secondary consumers, the meat eaters.

Carnivores other than coyotes prey on sheep, and these include wolves, foxes, mountain lions, grizzly bears, and golden eagles. In truth, predation comes from every conceivable direction. Warren Kelly, co-author of *The Desert Bighorn*, wrote ". . . The golden eagle soared up for another attack, while its mate struck the yearling. Four times each great bird zoomed and struck, always in the same place . . . Straight and fast as a bullet came the female bird, striking this time at an angle in order to get the sheep to fall."

Through the years others have witnessed predation by golden eagles, and at one time eagles were disposed of so that sheep might live. In the 1920s, National Park Service policy called for the elimination of predators so that the "good animals," such as sheep, might survive.

State agencies also practiced that policy. In Texas, in the 1920s and 1930s, game wardens carried rifles which policy demanded they use on eagles, killing hundreds over a period of years. Did such slaughter help? Did it increase herd numbers or strengthen the herd's intrinsic qualities? Responded one biologist in an official report, "It did not."

One of the most significant predators with which sheep must contend is the mountain lion. Though lions prefer deer, when deer numbers are down, mountain lions move to the domain of sheep.

Though lion predation often can be significant, most biologists believe that when considered as a whole, the effects are relatively small. The most telling of times would be when a lion entered into a sheep range with a small population, as in Colorado when a biologist saw a large lion on sheep range. In only five days the lion killed four sheep, which represented almost half the herd. Nevertheless, biologists believe that mountain lion predation only seriously affects herds with marginal population numbers.

Reports from other states also indicate mountain lions are the bighorn's most significant predator. In one 10-year study, researchers found that 66 percent of radio-collared desert sheep in Nevada fell victim to mountain lions.

Although stories of lion predation are common, what must be remembered is that coyotes, wolves, mountain lions, and sheep all evolved together, a fact some have difficulty remembering. In Alaska, one outfitter told me that each winter he watches wolves run sheep off cliff faces for the "sheer joy of killing." Others say they doubt such killings and have developed philosophies of their own. Said Mark Hinschberger, a biologist

Through the millennia, wolves have made sheep strong,
for only the very strong survive this predator, unlike this Dall sheep.

with the United States Forest Service in Wyoming, while speaking to a group of hunters, "The very characteristics we admire in sheep were derived from wolves." Hinschberger was referring to the elusive nature of sheep, and to their ability to evade predators by clinging to the sheer cliffs and rock outcroppings that deter all but the most stouthearted.

PARASITES AND DISEASE

Despite the fact that sheep are so incredibly well adapted to their environment and generally do elude coyotes, wolves, eagles, and mountain lions, few mountain sheep ever die of old age. If predators don't get them, often they are plagued from within by parasites. Because sheep are such social animals, when a disease strikes one, it strikes them all.

Biologists list over two dozen parasites that infest sheep. Some parasites are familiar, such as ticks, mites, and tapeworms. Some—like the bot fly and lungworm—are less familiar.

Sheep eat grass and, at times, when grazing, they also ingest lungworm larvae that cling to the blades of grass. After being released in the digestive tract, larvae reach the lungs by penetrating the intestinal wall and then actively migrate to the lungs. When they reach the lungs, the lungworms can eventually block off breathing. In advanced states, lungworms can cause asphyxiation.

One of the most extreme die-offs from yet another disease occurred in Yellowstone National Park when pinkeye infected a herd on Mount Everts. The outbreak occurred in December of 1981. Because the disease occurs naturally, park biologists did not interfere.

Animals afflicted with pinkeye lose their sight and tend to run in circles, often stumbling off cliffs and falling to their deaths. Before the disease had run its course, the herd of almost 400 had been reduced to less than 100. In 1996, the herd had climbed to about 230 animals, demonstrating that populations of sheep rebound very slowly.

Sheep may also weaken because of an infection in the nasal cavities, resulting from fighting. Or the teeth in their lower front jaws may drop out. On rare occasions sheep have died from porcupine quills. In the North, avalanches may kill them. If a predator does take a bighorn when it is older, the sheep may be considered lucky, for death is often a lingering affair, sometimes resulting from starvation.

Few sheep live past the age of 12, though there are exceptions. Collared sheep in Idaho, California, and Utah have lived to be over 20, but these are the exception.

Cliffs provide a stronghold from a multitude of predators that include eagles, mountain lions, coyotes, and bears.

Overleaf: Because of the debilitating effects of parasites, few sheep live past the age of 12. In death they become food for scavengers such as these ravens.

CHAPTER FOUR

PERPETUATING THE SPECIES

THROUGHOUT NORTH AMERICA, many species of wildlife engage in ritualistic contests to determine male order of dominance during the mating season. In the animal world, few contests are more vigorous or few rituals more complex than among mountain sheep. I have watched these mammals in many areas of North America and am always awed by the violence of their battles.

When two rams collide, the dynamics of motion are immense. Bodies telescope. Ridges and grooves of the horn tear out hair from opponents and often leave imprints. Necks twist and shock waves ripple along the animal's hide from front to rear. Often shoulders are broken and the regions around the eyes are torn. Horns are splintered, noses broken.

But it is the skull that sustains the greatest impact. By way of comparison, biologists have determined that in the course of routine battle, mountain sheep experience forces sixty times greater than that needed to fracture a human skull. Often, they experience these forces not just once, but many times—and in rapid succession.

Several years ago, my wife and I backpacked through Alaska's Arctic National Wildlife Refuge. In the endless daylight of late summer, we awoke one morning to the impact of a resounding crack. Peering from our tent, we watched what must have been a repeat of moments before.

Along the side of the nearby mountains, a large, full-curled ram backed to a distance of about 20 feet from another ram. Then it tilted its head as though assessing the other's reaction. For a moment the two stood silently, eyeing one another.

Like rams, ewes also possess horns that are retained throughout life, though theirs are smaller in circumference and much shorter in length. Ewes also possess some cranial adaptations that reduce damage from the fights in which they occasionally engage.

Without warning, the two rams simultaneously reared on hind legs, lunged, and ran forward to increase momentum. Seconds later, horns and skulls collided, cracking with a thud that broke the Arctic stillness as it reverberated from one side of Gilbeau Pass to the other. After the collision, the two again stood silently, dazed perhaps, but not subdued, for moments later the monarchs again reared into battle. Time after time they clashed, until it seemed as though their skulls and horns would shatter. Forty minutes later, the two wandered off, neither an apparent victor, the conflict of dominance for females and territory still to be resolved.

Other naturalists have recorded instances of evenly matched competitors clashing forty-eight times in a single day, seemingly with no ill effects other than fatigue—amazing, for when rams collide, they often do so with combined speeds of 50 to 70 miles per hour. Multiplying that figure by the weights of the two animals suggests a combined output of 2,400 foot-pounds of energy.

Sheep can sustain such blows if the collisions occur in such a way that built-in defense mechanisms are maximized. That's not always possible, and occasionally a ram will mis-time the moment of impact and catch the full force of his opponent's charge on his face; the result, a broken jaw, an injury that is sometimes fatal.

ADAPTATIONS FOR BATTLE

Through the eons bighorns have evolved a variety of techniques and physical adaptations to reduce the damage that might otherwise result from the force of each collision. Both males and females possess these adaptations, though they are more pronounced in rams than in ewes.

At the crown, the top of the skull is extremely thick with some cellular cushioning beneath it. For even greater padding, ossicones—a tough, gristle-like material—protrude where the horns attach to the skull.

Beneath the ossicones, two layers of bone connect with numerous bony cross sections—much like a honeycombed pattern—which further protects the brain. But there is more. All vertebrate skulls contain wavy hairline cracks called sutures. Mountain sheep have sutures that zigzag much more widely than do those found in other mammals. These sutures allow the plates to adjust when horns clash. This movement helps to absorb the shock at the time of impact. Researchers have determined that compression behind the horns measures more than twice the tension in front of the horns, meaning the sutures alone absorb half the force of impact.

The sheep's skull protects in yet other ways. Both horn cores are made up of a solid bone. So too are the bones around the nose. Also, when

Overleaf: Fights are often repeated and, in the extreme, have occurred as many as 48 times in a single day.

rams are about 3½ years old, a protective knob of spongy tissue begins to develop at the back of the head, and becomes more pronounced as rams grow older.

Muscle formation also protects the ram. In the neck, strong muscles anchor the skull to the neck. This support is particularly important when rams miss the exact mark and only one horn strikes its opponent, for as one biologist said, "the twisting force must be immense!"

Putting everything together, what we have is a horned animal protected further by a double-layered skull strengthened with struts of bone; thick facial skin; and a broad, massive tendon connecting the skull with the spine, an arrangement that allows the head to pivot and recoil with the blow. In a nutshell, we have an animal built to survive sledgehammer-like blows, not just once, but time after time after time.

BODY LANGUAGE

Generally, rams do not fight repeatedly. Such an effort would eventually take its toll, not necessarily on the skull, but on the ram's overall energy level. To prevent recurring battles, rams communicate their status in ways that they remember.

Rams communicate their status in a variety of ways, including "horning."

Bighorn rams rarely, if ever, make any sound, except to grunt or snort when angry, or gnash or grind their teeth. Instead, rams express themselves through a complex system of body language. At a very early age, rams begin prodding or "horning" one another with their horns as a form of communication. The need to do so is an inherited and inbred trait. As horns grow, young rams begin to associate the size of the horns with strength and power, all of which becomes imprinted during horning.

On the side of Mt. Altyn in Glacier National Park's Many Glacier Valley, I have seen the battles of young lambs throughout the summer, pushing and shoving one another with their heads and the stubs of their

A multitude of cranial adaptations enable rams to withstand 70 mph collisions.

developing horns. The impact of their blows is insignificant, but the information they attempt to transmit in these early battles is not. Through such testing, young rams evaluate one another's strength.

Rams continue evaluating one another throughout life not only by horning but in other, more complex ways. Rams may engage in brief clashes intended simply to reacquaint one another with a previously established order of dominance learned during horning. Immediately after the clash, rams raise their heads and turn them sideways, displaying their horns to full advantage. This move enables combatants to equate the power of a blow with the size of the horns.

Rams may progress through a ritualistic sequence of posturing, in which one lowers its neck and then stretches it out in an effort to make a formidable showing by maximizing the appearance of its horns.

If posturing fails to completely subdue the instinct to battle, increased physical confrontation can occur. A ram might make a threat jump. Or he might lower his head and point his horns toward his opponent, again to maximize the appearance of his horns. Another technique might be to horn an adversary in the side and continue doing so until the defendant becomes submissive. The dominant male then mounts the subordinate male as a further gesture of dominance. Biologists believe that such homosexual behavior occurs when a male has been displaced by a more dominant one. This behavior is one more technique that helps to generate a very recognizable social hierarchy among sheep, and this order is one that is created and practiced not just between males, but between females, and sometimes between a male and a female.

Throughout the bulk of the year, males remain separate from the ewe–lamb herd and they establish a dominance that supersedes all other herds. Nevertheless, a number of very significant developments occur in other herds. Invariably, within the ewe–lamb herd, a single ewe asserts herself, though this is a function of age—of wisdom, if you will—and not strength or horn size.

But in the fall, when males and females unite, a single male asserts himself over all others, though there remains a conspicuous pecking order that has been formed and then reaffirmed throughout the year, in part through "sheep talk." Some of the talk is performed often, is unique to sheep, and is highly visible not only to sheep but to sheep watchers as well. If you see it, you'll know exactly what the name describes.

The most common form of "talk" is the "low stretch," a social signal in which the head is held low to the ground and outstretched. Females occasionally use the technique, though males use it much more frequently.

In the fall, rams view one another through a pecking order that is often tested.

It is generally used to scorn another of the same sex. Males use the gesture to display horn size, thereby insulting a subordinate ram, often during courtship. For dramatization, rams may twist their necks during the low stretch in a gesture known to biologists as "the twist."

A final means of communicating overpowering strength that relies on horns is the "present." The present is a gesture by which a ram elevates his head, and hence his horns, in an attempt to display these weapons to greatest advantage. In an attempt to circumvent a battle the gesture often precedes a possible clash. However, the present always follows a clash of horns by the obvious winner and sometimes by the yet-to-be-convinced loser as well.

Rams also communicate toughness through the use of the "front kick," a practice that is unique among sheep, the gesture is performed often and will be recognizable. As a prelude to the front kick, typically a ram will barrel into its antagonist with its chest, then deliver a series of jabs with one of its front legs, often to one of the opponent's sides but sometimes to the genitals. The message, once again, is: "Hey! Don't mess with me!"

Sheep also communicate in ways that are not unique among sheep. They sniff one another and do so often. But sheep carry the sniffing one step further.

Often, rams engage in "huddles." Huddles occur most typically during the spring, summer, and early fall. They occur when rams group into a tight band facing inward, rumps pointed outward. Rams in huddles mix with a minimum of strife. As a means of recognizing one another, subordinate rams may chew a dominant's horn. At other times, all may continue sniffing. Sheep possess a preorbital gland located just below the eye. Secretions from the gland individualize animals and help them distinguish one from the other. When first meeting or while huddling, rams may rub their noses and horns against the preorbital glands, which provides identification, important when a subordinate meets a dominate, for such recognition reduces combat and injury—perhaps even death.

WHEN ALL ELSE FAILS

On a hillside, along the edge of a snow-covered cliff face, a belligerent male tramps toward another ram, approaching it from the rear. Raising its right front leg, the aggressive ram strikes down hard, raking his opponent along the rib cage. The attack brings little response, so the combative male tries another approach. Moving broadside to the subordinate, placing himself on the subordinate's left side, the attacker lashes out with his rear leg, punching the other in the stomach. Again, no response. Soon another ram joins the fray and the tide turns. Almost as though in council, the two subordinate rams appear to pass information and devise a plan of attack. They assume the offensive, somehow knowing that there is strength in numbers. Rearing back on hind legs, the two subordinates hurtle themselves at the aggressor and soon drive him away. Meanwhile, watching quietly—almost demurely—stands the object of all the fuss, a ewe that has come into estrus.

Though battles can occur at all times of the year, most fights occur when a ewe enters estrus. To time the 175-day gestation period so that birth coincides with the spring green-up, most fights in the north country occur in the fall. Biologist Kim Keating believes that in Yellowstone and Glacier national parks, the rut, with its allied battles, peaks around Thanksgiving. In the desert, because green-up has a broader window of time, estrus occurs earlier. And so do the fights. But whenever fights occur, they are a sight that generates a sense of awe, for these are primordial encounters.

The most serious fights occur among rams in the 6- to 8-year-old category. These rams usually have a three-quarter horn curl and are the ones attempting to establish a breeding status. As a prelude to battle, rams may push and shove each other as a warm-up to the main event. Strangely, they then turn and feed in opposite directions, seemingly oblivious to each other. Then, almost simultaneously, both turn and hurtle themselves through the air. At the last second, both rams drop onto their front legs, adding the force of gravity to their forward charge. Shock waves from the impact ripple back over their muscular bodies, dislodging loose hair and dust.

When mountain sheep collide, they do so with a killer-like determination. The noise from these collisions can be immense, like the crack of rifle fire, like the thud of crashing timber. Few other battles in nature seem as magnificent—as powerful—as do the collisions of two rams with massive curling horns.

Distinguished Canadian sheep biologist Valerius Geist, who has made a science of studying sheep battles, attributes the intensity of the force of impact to four components, which he says are additive.

First, rams begin the contest by rearing back, and from that point, the forces begin to mount. Everything from the drop to the final lunge enters into the equation.

Next, after rising on hind legs, the two combatants begin dropping down, simultaneously charging. Then, as the distance narrows, the rams lower their necks. Finally, they tilt the horns forward and collide.

Jack O'Connor, perhaps the most noted chronicler of the animal as a game species, likens the forces to that of a pitcher who arcs back, then drops forward, and then, finally, flicks his wrist to yet further increase velocity.

Sheep often cease fighting after just one blow, but not always. In Death Valley, biologists Welles and Welles watched two rams blast each other over forty times in two hours.

The "front kick" is an insult to a subordinate ram.

Others have watched even more intent rams. Photographer Michael Francis watched and recorded two sheep hammering away at each other along the side of a steep cliff. They fought for hours, pounding each other until exhausted. Still not satisfied, they continued the battle, locking horns and losing their footing, both plummeting to their deaths on the hard rocks below.

THE RUT

Fall is a magical time in the mountains. The leaves turn to gold, berries on mountain ash trees hang low, and snow begins to cap the mountain peaks. As well as characteristic sights, there are characteristic sounds, among them the recognizable ring of sheep still attempting to determine the order of male dominance.

Fighting among rams continues through the fall, and on days when the air is crisp and clear, the crash from these sounds can be heard over a mile away. Generally, these late battles occur when a ewe has entered estrus, or between rams from different bands. In the fall, rams are in peak physical condition, filled out and powerful, their bodies rippling with muscle. They are spirited, and nature has taken great pains to ensure mating will succeed, for the survival of the species is dependent on their success, which is encoded in their physiology and psychology.

In at least one respect, sheep are somewhat unusual

Overleaf: Sometimes several rams may "gang up" on a single ram.

among hoofed animals: rams fight for dominance of a ewe in estrus. Other species fight for harems or for territory. Antelope, for example, establish firm territories. Bull elk, on the other hand, form harems and fight with all their being to protect that harem.

Sheep, if anything, resemble deer and moose, with rams always moving from one group of females to another. In the course of a single day, deer, moose, and sheep may cover as much as 16 miles, traveling from one winter range to another, looking for a mate.

If several rams simultaneously find a ewe, she may be besieged by all of them. Even if the ewe is not quite ready, rams may plague her, giving chase

The "lip curl," or Flehmen exposes an opening in the sheep's Jacobson's organ. In turn, the organ informs the ram of the ewe's degree of receptiveness to breeding.

that may take the group from one mountainside to another. One researcher counted as many as nine rams in pursuit of a single ewe, the largest horned male leading the pack. All breeding that follows is performed at random, but by the dominant male. That's not to say subordinate males don't breed, though their success depends to a large extent on isolated chance encounters with a receptive ewe. If a ewe, however, prefers to remain unreceptive, she has ways of thwarting the males. She may back into the side of a cliff or tree, or jump onto the side of a cliff where there is but room for one. She may also lie on the ground.

When approaching a receptive ewe, a male may strut over to the female with outstretched neck in an effort to maximize the size of his horns. He may sniff her. She may then urinate on or near his face. Predictably he responds by raising his head and performing a conspicuous lip curl which exposes an organ located in the upper palate known as the Jacobson's organ. Curling the lip exposes the Jacobson's organ (vestigial in humans but pronounced in snakes and other reptiles) and simultaneously opens an orifice in that organ, telling the brain whether or not the ewe is in estrus. Though such facial display is practiced by other ungulates, the upraised lip is particularly pronounced among sheep.

Once a ram finds a receptive ewe he attempts to isolate her from the other rams. He may shoulder her toward a secluded series of cliffs, where courtship begins. A female may perform a coquettish jump. She may horn and butt the ram on his shoulder, or she may rub her body full-length along the body of the ram.

A ram may not mate just once or twice, but dozens of times. One researcher documented a single ram and ewe pair mating thirty-eight times—all in the course of a few hours. The duration of each union, however, is brief, perhaps just a minute. Survival in a world where predators always stalk demands a constant vigil.

Following the estrus, the ram moves on, for there is no fidelity among sheep. In the course of a single breeding season, a ram may breed with ten to twenty ewes.

Mating attempts occur among rams of all ages, though the most successful are 7-year-olds. This is the age when the horns of rams have obtained their greatest growth, and when rams are in the prime of their adulthood. A ram's success remains a function of horn size, and that, of course, is a function of age. Rams are sexually mature at 2 years old, but their status in the breeding hierarchy is low, because at this age, their horns are but a quarter curl.

Rams well past their prime also attempt to breed, and although their horn structure may be large, they lack the corresponding strength to maintain their hold as "King of the Mountain." As the years go by, they often seek a solitary hill, sensing that time has passed them by.

With the completion of the breeding season, sheep settle into difficult times. Ironically, the most aggressive and active rams are those that will have the shortest life span. They have exhausted themselves and must search hard for food. Ewes may not have it any easier, for most are now impregnated and eating for two. Like the rams, their most difficult challenge may simply be to survive the winter.

In a single day, sexually mature rams can mate literally dozens of times.

Overleaf: The physically superior Lothario may so deplete himself that overall longevity is reduced. Sometimes, surviving winter is a seemingly overwhelming challenge.

CHAPTER FIVE

GROWTH AND DEVELOPMENT

FOR WILDLIFE IN GENERAL, the most difficult of times is from birth until they are acquainted with their environment. Some species live in confined worlds that can be mastered quickly. Not so with mountain sheep. Their world is complex and often fraught with much trial and error and some death. Nor is the world easy for ewes that usher their young into this world and then attempt to nurture them as they grow and develop.

THE SAGA OF "BENT HORN"

The young ewe with the bent horn now growing toward her face climbed higher, unaware that previous generations had preceded her in similar efforts. Onward she climbed, ascending past the broad bottom slopes and up the loose rocks, past the surrounding wash where the terrain was generally clear and her vision sure.

Pausing for a moment near a small ridge, the ewe looked around and surveyed her world. Before her the land dropped precipitously, then joined with other slopes and rolled eastward, eventually merging with prairie and sky. But it was the undulating country near her that she studied most intently, and she focused on a clump of brush that flanked a narrow wash. She moved tentatively, approaching the shrubs one small step at a time. When abreast, she put on a burst of speed that was remarkable considering her weight. Over the past 170 days, she had gained 19 pounds.

With but rare exception, ewes give birth to a single young.

After passing the thicket, "Bent Horn," as she had come to be known by many locals, climbed even higher. She passed the receding snowbanks of winter where she had spent so much time munching the grasses that grew luxuriantly out on the flats, even in winter.

The 3-year-old ewe had no conceivable notion of what drove her up toward the rugged shale cliffs, but there was a gnawing in the region near her stomach and she felt weak. She wanted seclusion from her sickness. She wanted protection from the several grizzly bears she had seen the day before, and from the coyotes that yipped nightly. She wanted assurance she would be safe from an overhead attack. She wanted isolation, even from her own kind.

At last the ewe with the bent horn reached an enormous outcropping through which she began to thread her way, soon finding an overhang that satisfied her and her need for isolation. She pawed a depression in the ground and there she lowered herself and slept. When not resting, she occasionally moved to the tiny ridge where she snipped at the strands of grass.

Entry into the world brings challenges for both lamb and ewe.

On the fourth day, the muscles in her stomach began to bunch. Within the hour the head of a young lamb appeared, followed by the gradual appearance of the young's extended front legs. One last hard push ushered the entire lamb into the world, and for a moment the ewe remained silent. Then, lifting her head, she bleated, and struggled to rise. From the first appearance of the lamb's head until the time the lamb was on the ground, but five minutes had passed.

Though scientists never tracked Bent Horn by means of a radio collar or by a band marking her, she was easy to identify because of her horn anomaly. Probably she had sustained a fall when she was a lamb, for the downward twist of her horn occurred from near the base. Because of her unique horn formation she attracted much attention from those who saw her. Would the horn grow into the side of her face? If so, would it cause an infection from which she might not recover? And if it became a source of irritation, might not she simply reduce its growth by "brooming" it, as did the rams? All were considered possibilities.

Rangers, naturalists, and many locals followed Bent Horn through the years, and she never failed to appear. Each spring after winter released its grip and the roads were cleared of their heavy snow deposits, locals studied the hillside, searching as well for the young lamb the ewe invariably seemed to produce.

The story of Bent Horn is a true one, and undoubtedly parallel episodes have occurred throughout sheep country, for other ewes with bent horns have wandered the Many Glacier Valley of Glacier National Park, clinging to the side of Mt. Altyn, where coulees collect vast quantities of windswept snow. Here, one side of the mountain faces south and receives the warmth from the southern sun longer than do other mountain slopes having a different orientation. The area serves as an ideal winter range and, in the spring, as an ideal nursery ground, not only for Bent Horn but for dozens of other ewes.

This particular chronology is one I followed for half a decade, covering the annual appearance of this ewe for my small hometown newspaper, *The Bigfork Eagle*, drawing on events I observed and those I acquired from research. The saga of the ewe with the bent horn stirred sympathy, and the details of her life intrigued many.

Overleaf: In Glacier National Park and most other mountain strongholds, lambs are born at a time that coincides with the green-up of new grass.

INFANCY

Though no one ever saw the ewe with the bent horn giving birth, biologists have watched captive ewes and they know the details associated with labor. Ewes give birth while lying down, a luxury sheep have that some hoofed animals do not. Caribou, for example, give birth in open treeless areas and, unlike sheep, do so from a standing position.

Nature assists the ewe, protecting her from possible damage during the birth process. The lamb's hooves are soft, though they harden within the hour, and the young lack any visible sign of horns.

When born, the lamb is covered with hair and weighs about 8 pounds. Young lambs are mouse-colored with light rumps and sides that may be a brownish gray. Often they are toothless, though molars may be showing. After birth, the ewes nuzzle their lambs and begin to nurse them. The small lambs wobble beneath their mothers' stomachs, stretch their little necks, reach the udders, and suckle the vital nourishment contained in their mothers' milk, which soon helps bolster the lambs' immune system.

As a lamb begins to nurse, the mother licks it dry. The process of drying takes about twenty minutes and is all the time needed for the ewe to imprint her unique odor on her lamb. In the future, the ewe will recognize her young by its smell. Cleansing also helps diminish birth odor and protects the lamb from predators.

Though young lambs totter on their feet, they can easily wander the first day. Nevertheless, a lamb stays close to its mother, often seeking comfort from the terror of a passing shadow or strange noise by hiding beneath her stomach. Should real danger occur, the ewe and lamb generally run, though when cornered, ewes will often stand their ground, as in a case that occurred near Coaldale, Nevada, in which the ewe protected her lamb. In that incident, the ewe sliced an attacking coyote with her hooves and horns, eventually killing the predator.

Several days after giving birth, ewes return with their young to the growing ewe–lamb herd, which offers the protection of the group's "many eyes." Sites of these ewe–lamb bands are chosen well, so that sentinels in the band can see predators. When the band feeds, several ewes stand guard.

Lambs remain with ewes for 4 to 6 months, after which time the mother weans her young by simply walking away.

While in these bands, ewes frequently break from their rambunctious young, leaving them behind with a dry ewe or with another of the mothers who will nurse not only her young but the young of other feeding ewes as well. As a further safety valve, one ewe will often adopt an abandoned lamb should disaster strike its mother.

Bighorn sheep are generally silent throughout the year, except when with their young. Upon their return from feeding, ewes often call their young with a series of "blatts" that resemble the "baas" of domestic sheep. The call is faint, but if her young strays, she calls out loudly. Conversely, when it is time to eat, the young call out.

Though many lambs still retain remnants of their umbilical cords, within a week after birth, lambs are springing after their mothers. Development is quick, and within four weeks, the young assume the general configuration of small adults, though without horns. By the beginning of winter, lambs are about three-quarters as tall as their mothers and weigh about 80 pounds. Both male and female lambs have horns, though at this point, those of the male are already beginning to exhibit greater heft.

For lambs that make it through the first months of summer, there remains but one more hurdle. Ewes wean the lambs from four to six months after birth, at which time they simply walk away quickly after a few seconds of nursing—unlike female moose and deer, which physically chase away their young. Nevertheless, some lambs persuade their mothers to nurse them into the first winter.

THE WORLD AT LARGE

Lambs may be born during any month of the year in the desert, but in the North, nature demands that lambs be born during a narrower window of time, when winter slacks and luxuriant spring vegetation begins to emerge. Along the slopes of Mt. Altyn, in Glacier National Park, you can almost set your calendar by the appearance of lambs, which occurs around the first of June.

Much the same holds true in other areas of sheep country, but every now and then something unusual happens, and once again sheep prove their adaptability. For instance, in Rocky Mountain National Park, sheep normally give birth to their young in May. But in 1993, following an outbreak of pneumonia, biologists saw only one lamb among 380 adult ewes. That year lambs appeared in July, meaning that ewes had entered estrus a second time. However, the subsequent mortality rate was greater as the young had not been able to accumulate the much-needed reserves of fat before winter set in.

Though sheep populations can adjust in different ways, most biologists agree that the birth of twins is unusual. In fact, biologists believe that most cases of "twinning" really represent times when a lamb from one ewe has strayed to join a ewe with a lamb of its own. Nevertheless, examples of twins do occur.

Though nature sometimes changes patterns to ensure that populations survive, the best assurance of sheep survival results from sociological developments. Formation of a lamb–ewe herd is not only important for the protection afforded by many ewes, but it offers lambs the opportunity to play and learn to interact. Both male and female lambs begin to butt, not only at one another, but at trees and rocks. Butting is a form of communication and is an activity lambs carry with them into adulthood, for it tells sheep much about one another. Lambs that don't have this opportunity are handicapped, not only in the social sense but in the physical sense as well.

Young lambs need agility, particularly in the terrain found throughout sheep country, for the greatest cause of mortality among sheep is from falls. Miscalculated leaps during the first months are common. It's a learning process to jump from one area to another. Such is the rationale for suggesting that the horn curvature in Bent Horn resulted from a fall, though in this case, obviously, a non-fatal one.

In their third summer, young rams drift away from the nursery band and begin attaching themselves to different ram bands.

Within the herd, the death knell sounds as the summer progresses. In many areas, lamb survival may approach 90 percent, but as the harsh realities of life confront the lambs, the survival rate plummets. In the first month, cold rain may exact a high toll; or perhaps an eagle, wolf, or coyote has filled its belly. As a result, the survival number drops to 80 percent. And so it goes as the summer fades to fall and the autumn chills to winter.

One critical factor for survival during the first year is having an adequate supply of fat. Fat comes from the diet and it begins with milk, which is high in protein. Several weeks later, lambs begin adding grasses to their diet. The nutritional value of grasses is generally high in the spring, but only if weather conditions have been favorable. Sheep must eat enough high-energy food to build fat reserves needed to carry them through winter, when vegetation is often scarce. During such times, death occurs either by starvation or because some of the young are too weak to elude predators.

Nature is not always kind, and at times, the end-of-the-year survival figures throughout sheep country dip very low. In 1977, the survival rate at Wyoming's Whiskey Mountain dipped to 28 percent. What are these figures saying? Though no one can say for sure, sometimes they reveal an abundance of predators. In some cases they reveal the outbreak of disease. Of course, the percentages also reveal a brighter side, as in the Black Hills of South Dakota, where the final rate frequently approaches 80 percent. Typically, the figures are more in the order of 50 percent, though the rate must remain somewhere about 25 percent to sustain a population's growth. In Glacier, where sheep have been followed for decades, survival percentages have sometimes plummeted, but they have always rebounded. And rebound they must if the Park's mountains are to have bighorn sheep, for although sheep populations can survive periodic lows, eventually they must cycle back if the herd is to prosper.

"BENT HORN" POSTSCRIPT

Though no one ever found the remains of Bent Horn, the highly recognizable ewe appeared along the slopes of Mount Altyn in Glacier National Park for at least 10 consecutive years.

Following birth, ewes need several days with their young to promote bonding. Much mother's milk is needed to ensure the survival of lambs through their first winter.

Just which of the many young lambs that have now grown into healthy rams and ewes represent her progeny is unknown. What sheep watchers do know is that her death did not occur from an infection sustained from the abnormal growth of the horn, for Bent Horn stopped appearing along the slopes before the horn touched her face. Perhaps the horn never would have grown into her face, for in the latter years of her life, the horn assumed a more downward arc.

As with others of her kind, Bent Horn had become fertile by about 18 months of age, but didn't conceive until she was 3 years old. She lived to be about 13 and remained fertile throughout her entire adult life, for in the wild, no animal goes through menopause.

The mathematics of the generations are relatively easy. Bent Horn probably gave birth to 10 lambs. Of those, about half lived. Because the herd is a naturally regulating one, and because no epidemic disease occurred during her life, the growth is exponential. Bent Horn left behind a substantial legacy.

Excessive rain, slippery rocks, and predators from both below and above challenge the young. Odds for surviving these obstacles increase as the months progress.

Overleaf: Having survived the first few months, these healthy lambs have a good chance of successfully confronting winter.

Over the eons, sheep had used these corridors so frequently that the lines became etched in the hillsides in an indelible manner. Sheep have routes they use to reach areas they need to satisfy their specific needs, and their continued usage is what has made these trails so distinct. They are but a smattering of the trails found in many areas of the West and are the routes sheep sometimes traverse as they venture from one seasonal range to another.

RANGE

Home range is a biological term that attempts to delineate the area used by a species. Biologists have grappled with the concept, realizing that different species are limited by different circumstances. Home range is not a static concept customarily; it may vary for bighorn males and females, for young and old, and for all from one area of the country to another. To complicate matters even more, bighorns have a multitude of seasonal ranges within the home range. Together, these seasonal ranges comprise the home range. Once the ranges are established, sheep remain loyal to them throughout life. In other words, sheep that use an area one season generally return to that exact same area—and all other seasonal home ranges—season after season and year after year.

Rams, for instance, have a variety of needs, and to satisfy them they sometimes need as many as six seasonal ranges. These include a rutting range, a pre-rut range, a spring range, a salt lick range, a summer range, and a winter range. By comparison, ewes need four ranges, which biologists categorize as the spring range, the lambing range, the summer range, and the winter range. On the other hand, rams and ewes can sometimes get by on two seasonal ranges—a summer range and a winter range.

Summer range can be a massive area or it can be a small area. In the North, size often depends on snow cover, while in the desert, it depends on water availability. Movement throughout these ranges can also be great or small. In the desert, sheep may not move more than 5 to 10 miles from the place of birth. In Idaho, where detailed studies have been conducted, sheep that winter near the city of Challis on the East Fork of the Salmon River travel as much as 40 miles between winter and summer areas. These are the longest bighorn migrations in Idaho and some of North America's most substantial.

SUMMER

Attachment to a seasonal range might be considered to begin in late spring, with a lamb's arrival into the world, at which time it follows its

Overleaf: Above Glacier's Hidden Lake and across from Bear Hat Mountain a "bachelor herd" luxuriates in the greenness of a pasture that will strengthen them throughout the summer.

mother from the ewe's lambing range to her summer range. Summer range for the ewe–lamb herd is located high on the slopes of a mountain's edge. In Idaho's Salmon River country, it is a land characterized by Engleman spruce, white bark pine, and lodgepole pine. Labrador tea, mountain heath, and bear grass often flourish under the trees, especially near lakes and streams.

Summer range for rams is similar, but generally located even higher, where snowbanks are perpetual. Here it is not uncommon to see entire bands sunning themselves on huge snowbanks.

Bighorns luxuriate on these banks, basking in the security of a recessed cliff, where they can look out over the land's endless sweep. Several rams may congregate short distances from the safety offered by the cliffs where they study the landscape, using their "many eyes" to evaluate uncertain movements. Other than that, life for rams during the summer is carefree: when they are hungry, they feed; when they are tired, they rest. And here they remain, until other needs arise.

For rams in the bachelor herds, one of those needs may be for minerals. In Colorado's Rocky Mountain National Park, rams leave the luxury of their summer range and travel from Sheep Mountain several miles

The summer range in Alberta's Jasper National Park provides excellent habitat.

to Endo Valley to satisfy their needs for various minerals. As a separate group, the ewe–lamb herd does much the same. And so the pattern continues throughout the summer until autumn begins to encroach with its deteriorating weather.

FALL

Fall migrations are in fact often made in response to weather conditions. Because of the way in which sheep feed, snowstorms send sheep moving before deer and elk. Elk and deer forage on the taller browse while

Allies through the summer, relying on the protection of their many eyes to spot predators, this gregarious group of rams will disperse into smaller and often antagonistic groups in the fall.

sheep forage on the low-growing plants that can be quickly covered by a few inches of snow. When this happens, sheep must move, and when they do, they predictably follow age-old routes and trails.

Sometimes these routes take them down, other times up, as in a Glacier National Park study area evaluated by biologist Kim Keating. Keating says that in the course of tracking sheep over a period of several years, he discovered that while some groups do winter near the valley floor, some winter on the windswept ridges of 9,068-foot-high Apikuni Mountain.

"Indian summer" often checks sheep movements. But as autumn snows continue to pile, available vegetation becomes scarce, and sheep have no

choice other than to migrate. Moves may be gradual ones, with the herd simply drifting along a mountain range, wandering in accordance with the availability of winter forage.

Other factors influence sheep movements, and in the fall, they are associated with the rut. Females, oblivious to the males, seek fall grounds that have appropriate vegetation. Simultaneously, if the weather is unfavorable, males move to a pre-rut range that also has appropriate amounts of vegetation. The size of this pre-rut range is determined by encroaching snow that determines the availability of vegetation. But as the fall progresses, the males move on to the rutting grounds established by the ewe–lamb herd. Because sheep must, above all else, eat, this ground—or seasonal range—is sought out more for available vegetation. The rutting ground is where mating takes place, and it is here sheep play out their great dramas.

WINTER

Following the fall rut, bighorns are generally forced by weather conditions to move to their winter range. Generally, the area is located on south-facing slopes of a mountain, where the sun shines longest in the colder months. The exposed face is also buffeted by winds that sweep snow from the slopes. Under such ideal conditions sheep usually find food, particularly if the snow is soft and fluffy, for the amount of snow is not always as important as is its condition. A heavy crust may render a large area unavailable, or make life just plain miserable.

State Biologist John McCarthy remembers a period in the late 1980s when snow blanketed the winter range used by Montana's largest wild herd, the Sun River Herd, located about 100 miles south of Glacier National Park. Snow during that particular February week was followed by a warm rain and then, once again, by subfreezing temperatures. For several days sheep pawed the ice sheet and for once, they lost their incredible surefootedness, sliding long distances on their sides before once again regaining their balance. Miraculously, not a single animal died. But the conditions did prompt the herd to move.

Obviously the forage of winter range is in a state of flux, constantly expanding and contracting, forcing sheep to move to find vegetation that is not buried under several feet of crusted snow. As with most moves, a mature ewe often leads the way, trailed by the most dominant of males. She has ascended to this position of dominance and leadership by fighting other females. Though they too fight with their horns, altercations are much less brutal than are those conducted by rams.

Typically a wise old ewe emerges as the leader, one that is cautious, prudent, and vigilant. When something concerns her, she pauses and assesses the problem.

On this day, the matriarch pauses at a stream where dense clumps of brown willow leaves wall off her vision. Extending her nose, she stands motionless. Coyote tracks abound in the snow, and the wild, crisp air carries messages she easily deciphers. For several long minutes she remains poised. Finally, she scurries across the ice-covered creek, her hooves churning the freshly formed ice into shards.

Though the ewe communicates no message, others in the herd quickly follow. The memory of the old ewe has paid off, for once again she

Fresh snow initiates migrations to ranges with better conditions.

Overleaf: Winter range is generally located on a south-facing, windswept slope that exposes winter forage.

has led the band to safety. Simultaneously, she has passed on her knowledge of the proper route for others to follow. This is the information that helps protect the herd from making terrible mistakes.

Sheep pass down information from generation to generation. The information remains etched on a sheep's mind, despite some changes in habitat. In Glacier, ewes still lead their bands past sheep traps used by American Indians centuries ago, despite the Douglas fir that has encroached on these ancient migrational routes. Though sheep are nervous as they pass through this forested grove, they still follow the trails.

SPRING

With the warm winds of spring, the snows begin to recede and the land awakens, once again exposing pastures of grass. Simultaneously, glacier lilies and buttercups poke from along snowbanks, responding to the prolonged periods of sunlight. About this time rams drift toward their spring range as do members of the ewe–lamb herd. Sometimes the range for the two groups is separated by considerable distance. At other times, the range is one and the same but when it is, males tend to remain separated from the ewes and yearlings. Here the groups stay until the snow diminishes and the land opens further, bringing the herd full circle. Once again, ewes seek out their lambing areas, while rams seek complete separation from the ewe–lamb herd, isolating themselves into their distinct "bachelor herds." These are impressive groups, for bachelor herds often consist of a dozen or more rams. In Rocky Mountain National Park, the Mummy Range herd of bachelor rams typically varies from 12 to 22 members.

Rams often achieve separation with a suddenness, moving quickly to the summer ranges. Ewe–lamb bands do the same, for there is some degree of urgency. The movements render sheep vulnerable to predation, and so the trips between the ranges are made hastily, often in the course of hours. They return to areas where food and escape terrain abound. Eons of tradition direct their movements back to a seasonal range that is both uninviting to predators and abundant in vegetation. And so the cycle progresses through the other seasons.

Having survived the summer, this hearty lamb should endure inclement weather.

Overleaf: This mixed-aged "bachelor herd" of Dall sheep
rests together in Denali National Park.

CHAPTER SEVEN

MANAGEMENT EFFORTS

DEEP IN A CANYON located high in the Coso Mountains of California, the rising sun was transforming an already spectacular scene into one of even greater amazement. As the light intensified, a multitude of ancient inscriptions began to emerge on the canyon wall.

Deeper now in the canyon I could see images of bows and arrows, shaman and deer, but it was sheep that dominated. There were square-bodied sheep, round bodied sheep, inverted sheep, erect sheep, large-horned sheep, sheep inside other sheep. This was the handiwork of an ancient people best known as the Anasazi ("The Ancients"), who passed between these same canyon walls through which I now walked. In their petroglyphs they left a body of work that does more than inform of a long ago passage. Their rock carvings open doors on ancient history, for today, the rocks are saying that skillful Native Americans developed a widespread cult that revolved around sheep.

During the height of the cult, hunters fashioned bows by heating a pair of ram's horns until soft and pliable, then shaping them into two symmetrical halves of the bow. They joined the horns at the middle with a peg. Once strung, these bows were powerful enough to drive an arrow through a buffalo. In California, the Papago piled horns in the belief that they could control the wind. In the Pacific Northwest, the Tlingit and the Haida made superb horn spoons and ladles. In many of these cases, sheep provided the basis for a spiritual force.

Through the millennia, sheep have provided the basis for a spiritual force, just as they once did for the "ancients" in California's Coso Mountains who carved these petroglyphs.

That much of the culture is easy to fathom, for it is tangible. Nevertheless, archaeologists are prepared to go even further. They believe that ancient people so valued sheep that when populations of bighorns were abused, they attempted—just as we are doing today—to bring them back. In those days, hunters used the early science available to them; they used rock art. By chipping from the rocks images of the species they desperately needed, they would appease the spirit of the sheep and encourage a return through their "hunting magic."

Today, thousands of sheep petroglyphs and pictographs cover the rocks in many parts of the West. Because of these images, biologists can, in part, conceptualize historic sheep range. Based on this evidence, they are returning mountain sheep with confidence to areas inhabited before Europeans placed an exploratory foot on North America, and before, in some cases, the Native Americans hunted them out. The knowledge acquired from petroglyphs about lands sheep once inhabited helps biologists' attempts to reestablish sheep. Unfortunately, an even greater form of "hunting magic" may be needed before we can once again see sheep flourishing on all their former range.

In addition to a variety of natural hazards such as porcupine quills, sheep now confront plagues associated with the expansion of Europeans.

DISEASE RESEARCH

Only time will tell whether the "magic" now available is sufficient, for a history of tragedies continues to occur. One such story occurred in the spring of 1996. The story is short but poignant.

One day, a transplanted herd of 100 bighorn sheep wandered among the cliffs of Idaho's Hells Canyon, just as herds before them had done for countless centuries. The next day 30 magnificent animals lay dead, with the prospect of death looming large for all the others. These particular sheep had replaced a herd that a domestically introduced disease had killed only decades earlier. Despite biologist's efforts to save the unaffected animals, before week's end over 70 sheep from Hells Canyon had died from a disease that could be controlled, but unfortunately simply has not been.

"One morning the animals were just fine," said Dr. David Hunter, a veterinarian who also tends wildlife. "When it's so unexpected, you just want to cuss and rant and rave."

Hunter was referring to a disease that produces pneumonia. "Whenever you see a herd of dead bighorns, invariably you'll find a domestic sheep standing in its midst."

Hunter is just one of a multitude of men and women dedicated to preserving wild sheep and restoring them to their native habitat. The roster of bighorn devotees includes celebrities and politicians such as Bob Hope and Gerald Ford. What this heterogeneous group shares is the desire to preserve, protect, and perpetuate herds of mountain sheep. And that is part of the magic, for today management must of necessity include a charismatic—as well as a biological approach.

Hunter may be a leader in the biological pack. He is a chief researcher in the frustrating attempt to arrest a disease that produces pneumonia and that periodically runs rampant among wild sheep. Pneumonia in sheep is carried by a bacteria known as pasturella. Its host is the domestic sheep, and when domestic sheep are introduced into wild-sheep habitat, the outcome is tragic and predictable. Bighorns die, for their immune system did not evolve with domestic sheep and they have no defense mechanism against pasturella.

Recently, science has made a multitude of advances. By examining the arrangement and order of specific protein-laden amino acids, Hunter can establish which sheep are disease-free and therefore immune to the deadly bacteria. These are the sheep that will be used in future transplants. Because pasturella has killed entire herds, Hunter's findings should surely provide sheep devotees with much encouragement.

Overleaf: "Magic" will be needed to protect sheep from the seesaw of technological baggage introduced by Europeans.

FIRE

Other managers have also been making breakthroughs. In the historic past, fire generally purified bighorn habitat. But during the past century, public perception has been swayed to view all fire as harmful and detrimental. In fact, in a controlled situation, fires are necessary for maintaining an environmental balance. John McCarthy says Montana's Sun River sheep herd (once the nation's largest wild herd) would be larger if it weren't for the history of fire suppression. "Trees have closed in," says McCarthy, "and unless management drastically revises its plan, sheep will always be in jeopardy."

Fire opens the forest floor, and when it does, sheep use routes previously abandoned because tree-covered space had decreased visibility. The benefits of fire began showing up many years ago. Just two winters following a September 1974 fire at the East Fork of the Salmon River in Idaho, sheep dramatically expanded their habitat. In Wyoming, following prescribed burning in the Whiskey Mountains, sheep are again following ancient migration paths. By the early 1990s, they had expanded their range to the point where the town of Dubois began celebrating the fact that the surrounding mountains now contained the nation's largest wild herd.

Fire has also helped sheep in other areas of the country. In April of 1987, managers in South Dakota's Custer State Park burned timber on 235 acres of bighorn sheep winter range. Burning did exactly what it was intended to do; it stopped the spread of ponderosa pine onto a mixed-grass prairie, thereby offering sheep a greater area on which to feed.

Though biologists are restoring ancient migration corridors with fire, sheep populations still need help, for their numbers have dipped too low. The challenge is to reintroduce an animal intolerant of stress that must now confront a variety of diseases with which it has not evolved. Jeff Grandison, a Utah biologist who has studied bighorns for over a decade, recalls that so many sheep died following an introduction made into Utah's Zion National Park in July of 1973 they feared the herd had perished. Almost twenty years later, biologists in a helicopter spotted a herd of about 40 animals and his hopes rose.

"That doesn't mean the herd is safe yet," said Grandison. "It just means the worst of our fears have not been realized. We'll need to keep watching them, and maybe we'll need to bolster the herd."

TRANSPLANTING

Augmenting existing populations is difficult but absolutely necessary. Isolated bands have no way of diversifying their genetic makeup, and the potential for inbreeding exists. What's more, isolated bands of sheep seldom do well. Bands of fewer than 50 animals do not survive more than 50 years, and herds of 50 to 90 bighorns usually perish within 70 years. Historically, only populations of over 100 sheep survive indefinitely.

"What you must do," says Frank Singer, a biologist with the Biological Division of the U.S. Geological Survey charged with restoring sheep to park service–managed lands, "is saturate an area. Because of the many complexities, it takes awhile for sheep to get things worked out."

Saturating an area means transplanting, for no other management technique has been more effective. As a result of transplanting, desert sheep populations in the Lower 48 have risen from 1960 estimates of 8,100 to about 15,000. But that's just part of the good news. Mountain sheep now occupy portions of Texas, the Black Hills, and North Dakota—areas from which they had been completely extirpated. Again, that doesn't mean the herds are yet safe, for with expanding populations other factors enter the picture.

PREDATION

One complexity is the relationship between predators and prey, just now being investigated. As humans, we have modified the natural order of life in almost inconceivable ways. Consider mountain lions, one of the primary species to prey on sheep. Biologist John McCarthy, who has studied sheep and mountain lions, drafted a 1996 Environmental Impact Statement about Montana's mountain lions. He says the big cats are a concern in many areas of the Northwest, and by way of explanation offers a scenario that began over a quarter of a century ago.

In the early 1970s, mountain lions in Montana began to increase when they were elevated to the status of a game species. The new protective designation meant mountain lions could no longer be taken at random. Predictably, lion numbers grew. But the story is more complex, as are the implications for management.

In the hierarchy of predators, wolves dominate. When wolves are absent, lion numbers increase. If deer populations are negligible—perhaps overhunted—mountain lions turn to sheep as their major food source. It's that simple. Lions have swum across large expanses of fast-flowing rivers chasing sheep. In one area, a single lion took 30 sheep. With no wolves to chase lions off a kill—limiting their numbers by sometimes depriving them of food—lions may be part of an equation that never really existed in primordial times.

The challenge now is to manage all these species, and that falls into a relatively new quagmire, one known as biopolitics—something that really requires wizardry. Wolf managers know about that—but so do sheep managers, for ranchers and wild sheep have long been at odds.

BLM Help

In Idaho, much of the bighorn's original range has been permanently altered, but the remaining unoccupied historic habitats could support large herds of bighorns if ranchers and other land users would cooperate and keep their stock away from mountain sheep. Put in other words, we must demand that public lands be managed in ways more compatible for wildlife. Tom Parker and Michael Scott wrote in *Idaho Wildlife*, the state's official wildlife magazine, "The potential for increasing the distribution of bighorns in Idaho is greater than for any other big game species." That may be, but historically, those responsible for domestic sheep and wild mountain sheep have clashed frequently in Idaho.

Mountain sheep prosperity requires determined, dedicated men and women who don't walk the fence. Bureau of Land Management biologist Joe Cresto is a member of BLM's Bighorn Sheep Advisory Group. The group has met regularly since 1982 to exchange ideas on how to enhance bighorn management on public lands. Although the BLM has historically managed land following the confusing and often contradictory mandate of "multiple use," Cresto has seen progress. Over the past twenty years, many habitat improvement projects have been completed and there have been many favorable land-use decisions. In some states, managers have removed domestic sheep from bighorn habitat. Almost 80 percent of the West's desert bighorn sheep habitat is on BLM lands. Of that, nearly two-thirds of potential bighorn habitat remains vacant.

"I know we're going to succeed," says Cresto. "Bighorns are part of our heritage and Americans want them back. Sheep are part of our national heritage, and Americans want sheep back where sheep have always been. We've got the direction and mandates; we just need to apply them diligently when the opportunities arise."

"HOPE"

Jim DeForge is a sheep specialist with advanced degrees. He has the imagination and energy to make sheep into a cause célèbre, despite obstacles

Radio collars help biologists track introduced animals
and assess the relative success of transplant efforts.

unlike those found anywhere else in sheep country.

Deforge lives on the premises of the Desert Bighorn Sheep Institute, which he manages, located on the ever-expanding periphery of Desert Palm, California. The 30-acre complex is surrounded by a chain-link fence that penetrates 3 feet into the ground and barricades against coyotes and feral dogs. Inside the fence, Deforge supervises the raising of sheep in a condition as natural as possible for later placement into natural settings, particularly important in the southwestern extreme of bighorn range. There, sheep may be more pressured than anywhere else.

Currently, peninsular bighorn sheep range from southern California into the Baja Peninsula of Mexico, but their continued existence is in great jeopardy. Huge metropolitan areas surround sheep habitat, and their swell is like a tidal wave washing well beyond the high water mark.

To mitigate the problems, DeForge transplants the Institute's young of the year, and he does so with panache. At a 1996 fund-raising banquet hosted by the Institute, DeForge designated honorary member Bob Hope as the person who would name the center's first-born bighorn lamb of the year. Without a moment's hesitation, the entertainer named the lamb "Hope."

By choice of names, Mr. Hope revealed he was as clever as ever. But he also revealed that he knew much about sheep and their improved status in some parts of North America, where at least hope now exists.

Reintroducing sheep to former habitat may be one of management's best means of ensuring that huge-horned rams will continue to occupy appropriate terrain.

Overleaf: Almost two-thirds of potential bighorn habitat remains vacant.

EPILOGUE

When the little sheep "Hope" was a year old, he was placed in the San Jacinto Mountains and joined others throughout the great expanse of country in which sheep are prospering. And, so, Hope made it to the wild, where in many areas the signs of prosperity are quite evident. By evaluating the vigorous social interaction among sheep, the tireless bonding of lambs and ewes, biologists can predict long-range survival.

In more than one part of sheep country I have watched these mini-dramas, and have been overwhelmed by the suggestion of power, grandeur, and herd prosperity, for they suggest a latent power that still exists—a vitality that is free at last.

What I have seen and am trying so urgently to convey is the portent for vibrant, primordial populations of sheep.

High on the flanks of a mountain somewhere in the heart of bighorn sheep country, a small lamb trotted over to its mother. The ewe stood erect and offered the opportunity to nurse to her persistent young. For three full minutes the lamb suckled—a very long time that only lambs and ewes belonging to a healthy herd can sustain.

Later the invigorated lamb joined other robust lambs and, together, they romped in a way reminiscent of the herd that Death Valley biologists Welles and Welles had once studied. Several lambs reared back, making mock charges. Then the ewes joined in the play, swirling on rear legs, pivoting off their front hooves, clamoring up one cliff face and down another. It was all reminiscent of the way I had seen herds in Canyonlands, Arches, and Yellowstone—even along the Missouri River where the now-extirpated Audubon bighorn once romped.

Strong young provide much hope that mountain sheep may one day range again from the Arctic to the tip of Baja California.

Overleaf: Healthy animals have the energy to clamor along cliff faces and across rivers.

And then, in a way symbolic of only a healthy herd, two yearlings strutted onto the scene. Here were two beasts with muscles that rippled, despite the shedding fur and youthful countenance. Though their horns were abbreviated, the bases were large. Proudly, they moved back and forth across their stage of towering mountains cut by glaciers, capped with snow, and shrouded before me now by wind-driven clouds.

Had their ancestors really descended from the urials almost two million years ago, crossed the wave-battered shores of Beringia where they eventually forged their way down onto the scorching deserts of the Baja Peninsula? Had these animals with the magnificent horns really made these movements between surges of massive continental glaciers when the land was alive with wandering beasts of all descriptions?

Of course they had.

These sturdy sheep with the magnificent horns had helped pioneer the way and, often, other types of creatures had followed. But it was our mountain monarchs that forged that route, and it was they that settled so comfortably into some of the world's most overpowering land and made it their home.

Sheep remain a pioneer species.

APPENDIX

CLASSIFICATION

Mountain sheep are members of the family Bovidae and are in the sub-family Ovidae, or the sheep and goat family. Sheep differ from goats by having concave forheads, glands near their eyes and on their hind feet, ears longer than their tails, and horns curving laterally.

Mountain goats belong to the genus *Oreamnos* while mountain sheep belong to the genus *Ovus*. At one time, the genus included 18 different species, but in 1940, noted sheep taxononmist I. McT. Cowan reduced the number to 10.

The large number of subspecies that existed prior to Cowan's work was the result of a battle between the "lumpers" and the "splitters." Splitters tended to create a subspecies for minute variations while the lumpers grouped animals on similarities. Many believe the work of Cowan imparted a realistic approach to the taxonomy of sheep, for even now, many have difficulty differentiating between one subspecies and another. Nevertheless, there are reasons based primarily on horn size and coloration that are better delineated by retaining the current groupings.

Based on Cowan's work scientists have accepted the delineation of two species based on horn size. The taxonomic lumping of these northern species into a category designated "thinhorns" is unfortunate, for indeed, both the Dall and Stone sheep are mountain monarchs. Often, their horn sizes overlap with those of the bighorn, a fact that causes much distress among those who classify animals.

Sheep found in Alaska and parts of northern Canada are called the thinhorns (*Ovis dalli*), while those located to the south are the bighorns (*Ovis canadensis*). The Rocky Mountain bighorn sheep is further divided into seven subspecies as follows:

Bighorns

O. *c. canadensis*—Rocky Mountain or Canada bighorn, from mountains on the Bow River south through Colorado.

O. *c. auduboni*—Now extinct; once ranged throughout the rugged lands of the Missouri River drainage basin and on into North and South Dakota.

O. *c. californiana*—Found in the lava beds or rim-rock country of British Columbia, Washington, Oregon, and northern California.

Compared with their mountain cousins, the next four subspecies, or desert sheep, are smaller and have a slighter build, lighter color, wider flare of the ram's curl, and longer horns on the female. The average adult desert ram in good condition weighs 160 to 200 pounds; ewes weigh about 105 pounds. Desert ewes may remain in the rut for 6 months, though they normally remain in the rut about 1 month.

O. c. mexicana—Along with the Nelson's bighorn, this is the most prevalent of the desert subspecies. It ranges south from Arizona, New Mexico, and Texas as far south as Chihuahua, Mexico.

O. c. nelsoni—The smallest, most primitive and Dall-like in cranial and horn characteristics. It is found in Nevada, Utah, and California, where it lives in Death Valley, the hottest region of North America.

O. c. cremnobates—The peninsular bighorn, confined essentially to the Baja Peninsula, though a tiny population extends into southern California.

O. c. weemsi—The southernmost of all bighorn sheep, confined to the southern tip of Baja.

Thinhorns

O. dalli dalli—The common Dall's sheep, found from the Arctic Circle south to northern British Columbia.

O. dalli kenaiensis—The white Kenai Peninsula Dall's sheep, differing mainly in cranial features from the common Dall's sheep, found on Alaska's Kenai Peninsula.

O. dalli stonei—The black thinhorn sheep or Stone sheep, confined to northern British Columbia and the Yukon Territory.

POPULATION ESTIMATES

Renowned naturalist Ernest Thompson Seton believed that in the more pristine times of the late 1800s, bighorn sheep (exclusive of thin-horned sheep) numbered about 2 million. Based on habitat typing, scientists believe the noted nature writer (also founder of the Boy Scouts of America) may have been correct. Today, those numbers have been reduced for reasons detailed previously in this book. Numbers have rebounded from all-time lows, though in several states, it was necessary to reintroduce sheep following their total and complete extirpation. Canada donated much of the seed stock, though in some cases, seed stock came from Montana's Wild Horse Island.

The following list provides the number of sheep present and the area of greatest abundance (if determined or significant) within a Mexican or American state or a Canadian province:

Alaska—50,000 to 70,000 Dall sheep, prior to periods of heavy-snow winters of late 1970s and 1980s. Possibly 30,000 to 50,000 in 1996, though no biological censuses yet taken.

Alberta—6,000.

Arizona—6,000 desert; 500 Rocky Mountain.

Baja California—3,500 desert.

British Columbia—12,000 Stone sheep; 500 Dall sheep; 3,300 Rocky Mountain Bighorn; 3,700 California Bighorn, scattered throughout.

California—300 distributed in 5 herds; the largest is the Baxter herd located in the Sierra Nevada Range.

Colorado—4,030 distributed in 48 herds with those in and around Trickle Mountain, Sangre de Cristo, and LaGarita totaling highest. Sizable populations also exist in Rocky Mountain National Park.

Idaho—2,800 distributed primarily along the Salmon River.

Montana—4,890 distributed in 42 herds.

Nevada—6,700 distributed in 5 herds; Hell's Break herd the largest.

New Mexico—500 Rocky Mountain sheep, distributed in 8 herds; most in the San Francisco Canyon; 200 desert.

North Dakota—250 to 300 animals in 11 discrete herds, located in the Badlands of the Little Missouri River, which flows through the western portions of the state.

Northwest Territories—14,000 to 26,000 Dall sheep in the McKenzie Mountains; 1,500 Dall sheep in a population shared with the Yukon

Territories in the Richardson Mountains.

Oregon—1,007 distributed in 10 herds; mostly in the Hart Mountains.

Sonora—2,500 desert.

South Dakota—163 in Badlands National Monument; 163 in Custer State Park's Black Hills; and 150 other free-ranging sheep in the Black Hills.

Texas—325 desert sheep distributed in 5 populations.

Utah—200 distributed in 6 herds; largest number around Mount Nebo.

Washington—550 distributed in 9 herds; largest number on Aeneas Mountain.

Wyoming—5,000 distributed in 6 herds; largest number in the Whiskey Mountains.

Yukon—3,300 Stone sheep; 19,000 Dall sheep.

FOUNDATION FOR NORTH AMERICAN WILD SHEEP (FNAWS)

Exorbitant expenses for research require imagination. One organization has met that challenge. The Foundation for North American Wild Sheep (FNAWS) consists of a group of sportsmen dedicated to preserving and restoring sheep. FNAWS provided much of the funding necessary to research the Hells Canyon Sheep herd that experienced the immense die-off cited previously in this book.

Each year, in a variety of western states, dedicated hunters bid on a tag to harvest a trophy ram. Occasionally the bids approach extraordinary marks, as when a sportsman bid over $300,000. As Executive Director Karen Werbelow noted, "The money is above what normal licenses run, and every bit of the money goes back to the state for research." More typically, bids approach the $100,000 mark as they do frequently in Montana, Idaho, and Wyoming.

The bids may seem outlandish, but the group is dedicated to its sport. Without the contributions, much of the pleasure of watching sheep by those who don't hunt sheep, would be lost. The organization contributes to the betterment of sheep herds that are not necessarily hunted. In fact, it is appropriate to say that wherever sheep are in jeopardy, FNAWS has provided financial support. They have funded sheep transplants, prescribed burns, and studies on populations dynamics, herd quality, and water-hole restoration.

FNAWS funds not only traditional scientific studies, but several esoteric ones as well. They are funding research into genetics. Long-range projects include the continued support of research at Hells Canyon and help with wildlife management in Mexico.

For more information on FNAWS or other organizations working to protect wild sheep, contact the following:

FNAWS
720 Allen Ave.
Cody, WY 82414

Bighorn Institute
P.O. Box 262
Palm Desert, CA 92261-0262
(Devoted to preserving the peninsular bighorn.)

National Bighorn Sheep Center
907 West Ramshorn
National Bighorn Sheep Center
Dubois, Wyoming 82513
(Located at the base of Wyoming's Whiskey Mountains,
the center is devoted to restoring sheep and interpreting the
nation's largest wild sheep herd.)

In some places, bighorns were almost extirpated around the turn of the century. Because they (exclusive of thinhorns) now number about 52,600, biologists believe there is hope for the species' continued prosperity.

INDEX